LEADER'S
TOUGH QUESTION
GUIDE

TOUGH

QUESTIONS

LEADER'S

GUIDE

**WILLOW
CREEK**

RESOURCES

TOUGH QUESTIONS

BY
GARRY POOLE
AND
JUDSON POLING

FOREWORD BY
LEE STROBEL

ZondervanPublishingHouse
Grand Rapids, Michigan

A Division of HarperCollinsPublishers

Guides in This Series

Don't All Religions Lead to God?
Do Science and the Bible Conflict?
How Could God Allow Suffering and Evil?
How Does Anyone Know God Exists?
How Reliable Is the Bible?
Is Jesus the Only Way?
Why Become a Christian?

Tough Questions Leader's Guide
Copyright © 1998 by the Willow Creek Association

Requests for information should be addressed to:

🏛 ZondervanPublishingHouse
Grand Rapids, Michigan 49530

ISBN 0-310-22224-9

Interior photography by Studio 139

Printed in the United States of America

98 99 00 01 02 03 04 /❖ EP/ 10 9 8 7 6 5 4 3 2

Contents

Introduction

Welcome to the Tough Questions series. We believe that leading a group that explores the following tough questions is well worth the time and energy invested. Francis Schaeffer said, "It is not more spiritual to believe without asking questions. It is not more biblical. It is less biblical and eventually it will be less spiritual because the whole man will not be involved."

What kind of people will want to delve into this kind of small group study guide? The reality is that both believers and seekers have questions. Sometimes people come to faith but at a later point in time realize their foundation is shaky. You or people you know may want to gain a better knowledge about truths you've accepted for years. This would be a great curriculum to help you reinforce that foundation.

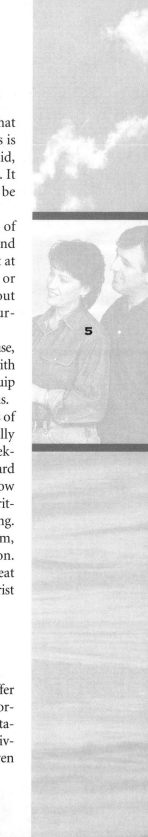

Others are interested in this series because they have a spouse, relative, friend, or coworker who has been hounding them with *their* tough questions. In this case, the group can serve to equip believers to engage in more productive evangelistic discussions.

Still others are seekers—people investigating the claims of Christianity to determine if it really is true. We're especially excited about the possibility that your group may include seekers because we know seekers need to have a safe place to be heard and get their objections and questions addressed. We also know from our own ministry experience there isn't a lot out there written to help a seeker investigate Christianity in a group setting. Whether you have only one seeker or a whole group of them, we believe this material is a perfect fit for such an exploration. The last guide in particular, *Why Become a Christian?*, is a great tool for helping someone cross the line of faith and receive Christ as forgiver and leader.

How to Conduct a Meeting Using This Material

Whatever the profile of your group, we would like to offer a few cautions for you to consider as you begin. First, it is important for you and your group members to have realistic expectations for your group. These guides do not cover every conceivable tough question, and you can't possibly answer in detail even

the questions they do explore. While they will help you and your group members make great strides toward satisfying answers, studying these issues is a lifetime endeavor. Additional reading will almost certainly be required for anyone to feel that he or she has a firm handle on the answer to any of these questions. So let your group members know that the group discussions will help them on their journey but they won't tie up every loose end.

Second, we firmly believe in a process that honors people where they are right now—even if they have "wrong answers." People need to know that when they come to the group they will be loved and accepted, even with their unorthodox beliefs. Incorrect answers need to be heard, in part for comparison purposes and also because we need to value each other even when the other person is wrong (someday, we may want the favor returned!). Paradoxically, when people feel the freedom to say what doesn't make sense to others, they become more open to what others have to say. This may also include a new appreciation for the answers provided to us by God in His Word. Our experience has shown us that minds change more easily when they are free to explore.

Third, we believe that your group should not become purely academic. If all you do is talk about questions and answers without also entering into a sense of community with the other group members, you will miss an important dynamic that is life-changing. That is especially true if you have seekers in your group. We've observed that people are more often repelled by Christianity because of the way they've been treated by believers than by the inadequate answers they've heard from those believers. While this is a generalization, we believe the Tough Questions series provides a tremendous opportunity for seekers to receive both good answers and a taste of loving Christian community. These are powerful tools in the Holy Spirit's arsenal to win back wandering souls. As the leader, set the relational temperature for your group. Make it a family, not just a class.

Finally, we caution leaders against adopting a know-it-all attitude. These people have not joined your group to hear your wisdom each meeting; they've come to discuss and explore together. Resist teaching, and instead lead a process of discovery. You don't have to have all the answers, and it will be better for all concerned if each person gets a chance to have his or her say. Over time, complete answers will begin to emerge from the collective discussion rather than from the brilliant mind of any one person in the group.

The Introduction

At the beginning of every session is an introductory section, usually several paragraphs long. Some group members will read this beforehand on their own, but we recommend taking time to read this together at the beginning of every meeting. We suggest that you vary how this is done from week to week. One week have an individual read it out loud; another week members can read it silently. You can also go around the circle and have each member read a paragraph.

The introductions are written from a skeptical point of view. Many of the freestanding quotes early on in the session also have a skeptical tone. These readings should help the believers in your group to feel the force of the tough questions people ask. Most people have known someone who has raised similar questions, and some have raised them themselves. If you're leading a seeker group, there will probably be a skeptic or two, so this information will help them feel understood and valued.

The introductions are also meant to be provocative. These are, after all, tough questions, and people should squirm a little in their chairs when they face them.

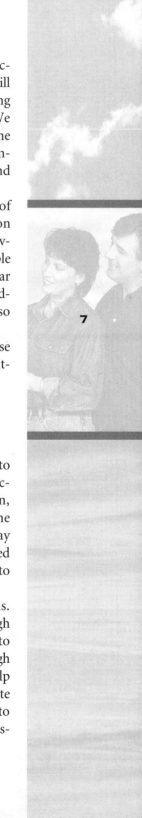

7

Open for Discussion

After you have completed the introduction, it is time to get into the meat of the session: the questions. We don't recommend that you force everyone to answer every question, because some people will feel uncomfortable and put on the spot. Encourage those who want to answer to do so, but pay attention to those who aren't participating. As a leader, you need to be sensitive to those who are quiet and help draw them into the discussion—without being threatening to them.

Most sessions contain from eleven to fifteen questions. You may find that it is difficult for your group to get through all of these questions. That is fine. The important thing is to engage group members in the topic at hand—not to get through every question. There are two extremes that leaders must help their groups avoid: the first, a regimented attempt to complete every question, as if the session is an end in itself; the second, to allow the group to get off on tangents and not get to the questions that everyone is there to discuss.

The questions in these sessions are designed to draw people out and to give them the opportunity to process things out loud. As a leader, your role is to facilitate that self-discovery process. While it may be tempting to short-circuit that process and give quick answers to very difficult questions, we believe that letting people live with the tension of those unanswered questions will eventually lead them to embrace satisfying answers that they discover on their own, rather than being force-fed by the leader.

People need to struggle with the questions deep in their souls—not just with the superficial questions toward which everybody gravitates. Whatever you can do as a leader to discover those deeper issues and engage people in discussion of them will be positive for the group.

Opening Question

Usually the first question of each session is an "icebreaker." Icebreakers are meant to get the conversation going by discussing a less threatening issue, usually one having to do with past experiences or common opinions. Starting each meeting with a more lighthearted, "personal interest" question is a good way to ease into the topic. It helps people bridge the gap between what's been going on in their lives "out there" and what needs to happen in the group meeting.

Actually, many of the questions in each session are designed to get people talking about themselves, not just about the issue at hand. This is an important group dynamic because it builds trust among group members. Don't overlook this important aspect of what makes a group discussion work. Allow people to share their stories in a nonjudgmental atmosphere and respect them no matter where they are on their spiritual journey.

"Straight Talk" Boxes

Every session has at least one paragraph called "Straight Talk." These are meant to be read by the group at the time of the session. As with the introduction, try to use a variety of approaches for reading these out loud. The question immediately following a "Straight Talk" almost always refers to the material just presented, so it is important that group members read the "Straight Talk" before they answer the question.

Miscellaneous Quotes

Scattered throughout every session are various boxed quotes, many of them from skeptical or critical points of view. These are intended to enhance the session, but are not necessary to answer the session's questions.

Heart of the Matter

The section called "Heart of the Matter" represents a slight turn in the group discussion. Generally speaking, the questions in this section speak more to the emotional side of the issue, not just the intellectual side. Part of the philosophy behind this series is the recognition that people have emotional as well as intellectual needs. God can and does meet both. As a leader, you need to help your group members find satisfying answers for both their minds and hearts.

Charting Your Journey

The purpose of the "Charting Your Journey" section is to help group members go beyond a mere intellectual discussion to personal application. This group experience is, after all, a journey, so each session has at least one section devoted to helping people talk about their current position. Those views will probably change over the course of this study. One function of this section is to help people see that change, and to recognize the transformation.

Conclusion

We believe that you, as a leader, are on just as much of an adventure as those in your group. We encourage you to pray for each member and stretch your own limits of learning. Without you, this group wouldn't happen, so it's our hope and prayer you'll feel God's commendation as you step into this role. May His power make your Tough Questions group a place where truth and love meet in perfect proportions.

—Garry Poole and Judson Poling

How Does Anyone Know God Exists?

11

Session 1: Is Anybody Out There?

Short Answer: Yes! Not only is He out there, He is personal, He cares, and He is reaching out to you.

Question 2 One of the most significant factors affecting our view of God is the image of our parents—whether good or bad. Things they said or didn't say and did or didn't do probably made an impact on us that lasts to this day. Another notable influence might be respected (or otherwise) authority figures. Peer pressure may also have contributed to our thinking about God, as well as things we observe in nature, books, and other information we have gathered from people we respect. Our consciences also tell us something about God.

There are at least two reasons why we have asked these questions: the first is to assist you and your group members with learning more about each other; the second, to build bridges of trust between the members of the group. It is important for group members to develop and maintain respect for each other, regardless of where they are in their spiritual journey.

Question 4 Most people are unintentional or haphazard in how they arrive at their view about God. It is important for them to see the reasons behind what it is they believe. This question can help people see that most don't have substantial reasons to back up what they believe about God.

Question 6 In many cases this will be the very first time group members will have ever been asked to describe their confidence level about what it is they believe. This may make some uncomfortable. Still, part of building a good foundation for belief is to recognize the crumbling concrete of the existing spiritual foundation, so that there will be a new readiness to find a way to build a stronger one. It is important for members to feel the freedom and safety to share their true thoughts and uncertainties in the group and not feel judged or put down in any way for what they do or don't believe. In his book *Asking God Your Hardest Questions*, Lloyd Ogilvie, one-time Chaplain of the U.S. Senate, asserts, "Johann Wolfgang von Goethe once said, 'Give me the benefit of your convictions, if you have any, but keep your doubts to yourself, for I have enough of my own.' I don't agree with that. I want to put it differently: Give me your doubts. Be honest enough to admit them. Our Lord is pressing us on to new growth. Our doubt is our human response. He can take our struggle with doubt and give us the gift of faith to ask for wisdom."

Question 8 The point of this question is to help group members see that they exercise faith all the time, not just in spiritual matters. Every day, people put their trust in things without assessing the trustworthiness of the object of their confidence. What makes trusting God difficult is that God is not tangible, whereas these everyday things are. R. C. Sproul states in his book *Now, That's a Good Question!* "I don't think there's anything that makes living the Christian life more difficult than the fact that the Lord we serve is invisible to us. You know the expression in our culture 'Out of sight, out of mind.' It's very, very difficult to live your life dedicated to someone or something you cannot see. Often you hear people say that when they can see it, taste it, touch it, or smell it, they'll believe and embrace it, but not before. This is one of the most difficult problems of the Christian life: God is rarely perceived through our physical senses." But God does give reliable evidence of His existence and trustworthiness, and this series is about discovering that evidence.

Question 9 Possible answers include the reputation of the person or company you are trusting (i.e., credentials, training, title, research, appearances, past experiences). Note: Lack of trust is also based on these same factors.

Question 10 Many people assume that if God were to show up and speak to them, then they would believe. They might also want answers to prayers and other evidence that God is showing His favor on them. A more intellectual type may ask for historical evidence or scientific proof. Note: As a leader, be sure not judge what appears to be a foolish or inadequate answer.

Question 12 This question will draw out group members' different personalities, styles of interaction, and discussion preferences. Pay attention to the sensitivities of the different group

members so that you can more effectively respond to them individually, as well as in the group.

Session 2: How Can Anyone Be Sure God Exists?

Short Answer: We may not be able to have *absolute* certainty, but we may have *reasonable* certainty.

Question 2 Press your group members to go beyond describing influences to giving concrete reasons that could persuade someone else to adopt their point of view. As we pointed out in the previous session, people tend not to have compelling reasons for belief—they tend to just believe something without stopping to examine why.

Question 3 For those who are concerned with proving God "scientifically," this question can help them see that the realm of science can't conclusively answer the question.

Question 5 Do not feel the pressure to address all the issues raised as a result of this question. At this point, just let group members express their doubts and questions.

Question 6 Don't get sidetracked or bogged down by this question. Experience shows that these arguments don't make or break someone's belief or disbelief in God. They are helpful, but often not conclusive.

Question 7 We recognize that, for some, these arguments are helpful; but for others, questions still remain. The good news is that God meets us at our point of need, whether that be intellectual, emotional, or in whatever area we're struggling.

Question 9 One possibility is that they would not have the anxiety and tension brought about by being plagued by doubt. Gullibility is not commended by God, but trust can lead to contentment and a secure relationship with Him.

Question 10 This exercise might be frightening to some group members. Do not force group members to take part in it.

Question 11 One of the main reasons people struggle with God is the terrifying view they've adopted of Him. As a leader, one of your tasks is to help people see the God who is really there, not the God of their fears. The next session will actually address our distorted views of God and try to give a clearer picture of Him. "Because God has spoken and has revealed Himself, we no longer have the need or the option of conjuring up ideas and images of God by our own imaginations. Our personal concept of God—when we pray, for instance—is *worthless* unless it coincides with His revelation of Himself" (Paul Little, *Know What You Believe*).

Question 13 Take note of each individual's response in order to help encourage each one's spiritual journey.

Session 3: What Is God Really Like?

Short Answer: God is better than you ever imaged Him to be, and the clearest picture of Him is Jesus.

QUESTION
ONE

14

Question 2 As a leader, this question and the one following can help you learn more about the people in your group. This information can be helpful as you encourage them on their spiritual journey.

Question 5 The enthusiasm a person feels toward the idea of getting to know God is dependent on what that person knows or believes about God's attributes: Is He someone the person would enjoy knowing? Also of concern is what a person feels God would provide: What needs might He meet, or what benefits will He bring? This may sound selfish, but it's probably an accurate gauge of the primary motivation behind a person's search for God. A. W. Tozer once said, "What we believe about God is the most important thing about us."

Question 7 The feathers in the analogy represent our opinions, which are weak ("featherweight"), while we mistake them to be strong (solid, reliable). The wind (reality) has the power, not the feathers. Many people consider their opinions to determine truth, when in fact, truth stays the same regardless of our opinions. In their book *Christianity Made Simple*, David Hewetson and David Miller admit that "we are more at home with our own ideas about religion—with thoughts which are more comfortable and reassuring, with a 'God' who is rather like us and who can be brought into line with our own expectations. This God is domesticated—like a religious 'pet', rather than the wild, untamed presence of the Almighty."

Question 8 The attributes are listed previously in the session in the Straight Talk "What and Who God Is." When you go through this question, people do not need to answer it for all six areas listed; just pick one.

Question 9 Be sensitive to those who might be offended at being compared to the devil. This question is not meant to judge them or make them feel bad, but to expose their faulty confidence; it is geared toward helping people discover that believing in God is not enough. Don't try to artificially ease the tension if someone recognizes the distance that exists between them and God.

Question 10 This question is a development thought from Question 9. It goes a step further, making it more personal.

Question 11 This question is similar to Question 11 from the previous session, but it focuses on the changes that are presumed to occur if the person becomes a follower of Christ. Many people have an exaggerated view of what Christians are like and are fearful of becoming one of "them."

Question 13 Prayers reveal the heart of a person; they also show the way the person approaches God and what they think of Him.

Session 4: How Can Rational People Believe in Miracles?

Short Answer: A God who created everything is a God who can do miracles. The whole question of miracles hinges on the question of God.

Question 3 People who refuse to acknowledge the possibility of miracles may not claim to be atheists, but by denying this aspect of God's power they accept a drastically altered picture of God. They may end up living like atheists, because they believe God doesn't get involved. Deists, for example, acknowledge God but believe He does not act in the world. Such a view is certainty not true of the God of the Bible.

Question 4 Paul Little, in his book *How to Give Away Your Faith*, answers the question of miracles this way, "The real issue is whether or not God exists. If God exists, then miracles are logical and pose no intellectual contradictions. A friend of mine who grew up in Asia once told me he just couldn't quite believe that a man could become God. I saw his problem in a flash and said, 'I'd have quite a time believing that, too. But I can easily believe that God became man.' There's all the difference in the world between these two concepts. By definition God is all-powerful. He can and does intervene in the universe that he has created."

Question 5 Christianity is a religion grounded in events that actually occurred. Something as unusual as a resurrection requires extraordinary support; therefore, eyewitnesses help authenticate Christian belief. Multiple eyewitnesses give that much more credibility. Those who would explain the resurrection as a hallucination must explain how five hundred people could have had the same hallucination simultaneously.

Question 6 Your group members will probably describe unusual or unique experiences, but based on the discussion up to this point, you need to ask what is the evidence of that experience being a miracle instead of just an extraordinary (but not divine) occurrence.

Question 7 The thought of miracles is really quite frightening. Many times when an angel appears to a person his very first words are "fear not." True miracles create fear.

Regarding the second part of the question, people may feel anger or sadness because they desperately want God's help but haven't received it the way in which they were hoping they would. Assure group members that it is perfectly natural to be emotional about God's apparent indifference.

Question 8 Miracles point to Jesus and His uniqueness. They are not common in our life, but they validate the extraordinary Son of God. Even though we are twenty centuries removed from Jesus' miracles, their "sign value"—the way they point to Jesus' uniqueness—still underscores His incredible life.

Question 9 If you are determined not to believe, a miracle won't change your mind.

Question 11 The basis of Christianity is the resurrection, which is, essentially, a miracle.

Session 5: Does God Care What Happens to Us?

Short Answer: Yes, so much so that He sent Jesus to bring hope into our world of hopelessness and despair.

Questions 2 and 3 Don't take a lot of time on these questions; the real punch comes when you discuss Questions 4, 5, and 6.

Question 4 The answer is the same for all three: people and God.

Question 9 Be sure to have these passages earmarked before the meeting and either read them out loud or have someone read from your Bible so you don't embarrass those who might not be familiar with the Bible.

Question 10 God's love is constant, but that doesn't mean we always feel it. Guilt can make us feel unloved, as can seasons of pain or confusion, but God's love is still there. Our subjective experience of His love is not the same thing as the reality of His never-ending love. In his book *Give Me an Answer*, Cliffe Knechtle notes, "The wonderful promise of Scripture is that God is bigger than anything we can do that's wrong. God can reach deeper than any pit we can dig for ourselves. We cannot commit a sin that God cannot forgive."

Question 12 Christians often make it sound as if God is a vending machine: I'll do this and He will respond and then I will feel loved. The reality is that God *does* do wonderful things for us, but He provides blessings that are more enduring, such as the forgiveness of sin and the promise of heaven. His love is not contingent on our getting every wish granted.

*How
Does
Anyone
Know
God
Exists?*

17

Session 6: How Can a Person Get to Know God?

Short Answer: We come to know God by recognizing the way of salvation He's provided and taking it.

Question 2 In a group where there are a number of seekers, this question will allow them to talk with Christians about their experience. This question also gets at the idea that there is a difference between concluding God exists (which is an intellectual matter) and getting to know Him personally (which goes beyond mere knowledge).

Question 4 The barrier is not an informational barrier; it is a sin barrier. Be sure to have this passage earmarked beforehand so you can read it (or have someone else read it).

Question 5 God loves those who are running away from Him. The fact that they have shunned Him has not stopped Him from loving them.

Question 6 It is about being lost and experiencing the void, even though you are physically alive. It means living in a spiritually dead position.

Question 8 In this verse, Jesus defines eternal life as knowing God. This verse is saying that there is no eternal life without a relationship with God, through Jesus Christ.

Question 10 Ralph Waldo Emerson described the impact of God's creation on him when he stated, "All I have seen teaches me to trust the Creator for all I have not seen."

Question 11 Many people's religious training has taught them lists of rules to keep, or behaviors that God wanted, or the importance of holding correct beliefs about God. That training never helped them see that God wants a day-to-day relationship with Him. For others, spiritual life was an automatic thing, whether they wanted it or not; they were never taught about the need for a conscious, deliberate decision to receive Christ.

Question 13 Spiritual life, like biological life, must be nurtured and cultivated. Spirituality thrives in an atmosphere that contains such things as living in community, honestly facing doubts, learning more about God and His Word, and conversing regularly with God (prayer).

Is Jesus the Only Way?

Session 1: Who Was Jesus?

Short Answer: Jesus is the most unique man who has ever lived; the Son of God, Savior of the world.

Questions 4 and 5 People usually never think about why they believe what they believe about Jesus. Failing to critically examine what sources have led to opinions is as dangerous as never examining those opinions. The reality is that many of us have based our eternal destiny on very precarious sources of information, and though our opinions might be strongly held, they are often weakly supported.

Even though this question may expose group members' weak positions, be careful not to allow members of your group to express negative judgments of each other. Encourage members to accept one another in spite of differences in beliefs.

Question 6 One of the ways to see how striking Jesus' claims are is to imagine someone you know saying the same things. You would be very uncomfortable indeed to hear a friend, coworker, or even the minister of a local church make these incredible claims. As P. T. Forsyth noted, "These claims in a mere man would be egoism carried even to imperial megalomania" (*This Life and the Next*). Yet Jesus was the supreme model of meekness and self-sacrifice. In his book *Basic Christianity*, John R. W. Stott claims, "The most remarkable feature of all this self-centered teaching is that is was uttered by one who insisted on humility in others. He rebuked his disciples for their self-seeking and was wearied by their desire to be great. Did he not practice what he preached?"

Some of the conclusions you could draw out of these verses include:

- He said God won't accept you unless you accept Him (Jesus).

19

- He said He has to be more important to you than even your most intimate family relationships.

- He said you have to love Him even more than you love your own life.

- He said He was on equal footing with God, being over the Sabbath requirements (like God) rather than subject to them.

- He claimed to have existed before Abraham, using the phrase "I am" (not the expected "I was"), which was a term God used (see Exodus 3:14).

- He said that if you'd seen Him, you'd seen God.

- He categorically admitted at his trial that He was the Messiah and the Son of God.

Question 7 On what basis do people think they know better who Jesus was two thousand years after the fact than the eyewitnesses who spoke to Him or to those who knew Him? The audacity of modern people willing to rewrite the story of Jesus with absolutely no factual basis is astonishing! (Malcolm Muggeridge notes, "It is not that people believe in nothing—which would be bad enough—but that they believe in anything—which is really terrible.")This question will hopefully show any group members who are doing this that they really have no evidence for reworking Jesus' claims other than their subjective personal prejudice. (Simply allow this question and the answers given to help group members discover this about themselves.)

Question 8 People resisted what Jesus said about Himself. Even His followers struggled with understanding exactly who He was. The fact that He asserted His unique role and identity in so many and various ways is strong evidence that these are not the additions of followers but His actual claims.

> It is not possible to eliminate these claims from the teaching of the carpenter of Nazareth. It cannot be said that they were invented by the evangelists, nor even that they were unconsciously exaggerated. They are widely and evenly distributed in the different Gospels and sources of the Gospels, and the portrait is too consistent and too balanced to have been imagined.
> —John R. W. Stott, *Basic Christianity*

Although we don't get into it here (see Tough Questions guide *How Reliable Is the Bible?*), there is ample evidence for the reliability of the gospel records, another reason to have confidence that the claims we read are virtually identical to Jesus' actual statements.

Question 10 Some people will be very comforted by the realization that Jesus clearly spelled out who He was, and that God loved them enough to send His Son. That very same reality will make others uncomfortable. Some may be angry because of the apparent narrowness of Jesus' claims. Be prepared for a range of reactions. Note: A good leader learns to be a good listener during these moments and patiently encourages members to feel comfortable sharing their honest answers.

Question 11 Our salvation is dependent upon knowing and affirming the true identity of Jesus. You cannot be saved from the penalty of sin without acknowledging your need for a Savior. You cannot enter the Kingdom of God without acknowledging its King. You cannot be forgiven sin without a relationship with the One who forgave you.

Session 2: How Is Jesus Different from Other Religious Leaders?

Short Answer: Though many other great religious leaders gave wisdom for living life, none made the radical claim to be God in the flesh and the only forgiver of sins—and none rose from the dead.

Questions 2 and 3 People often hold a religious opinion with a tenacity and smugness that exposes their underlying spiritual bigotry. Christians are not exempt from this fault. To say, "I have the truth because I'm smart and have figured it out, and you're wrong because you're not as enlightened as me" is arrogance, even if you do believe the right things about Jesus. But when a Christian humbly admits that it is Jesus Himself who compels us to affirm His uniqueness, that is not bigotry, it is simply handling the claims of Jesus with accuracy. Note: When members of your group describe people with unreasonable convictions, don't allow them to use actual names, and don't permit ridicule.

Question 7 Jesus could have been wrong, and His narrow-mindedness evidence of egotism or sincere self-delusion. But if Jesus was right, He wasn't narrow-minded. There's nothing narrow about the God of the universe saying, "I'm the God of the universe." That's a simple fact. What's narrow is a leader saying "I'm the only truth" when there are lots of other sources. Jesus is saying, "Whatever good any other person can do for you, *no one can save you except me.*" Oswald Chambers observed, "We can get to God as Creator apart from Jesus Christ, but never to God as our Father except through Him" (*Christian Discipline, Vol. 2*). If that is really true, Jesus words aren't limiting—they're a statement of warning, love, and safety.

Question 8 The possibility of misunderstanding has to be granted, simply because we're finite humans, who can be mistaken. But Jesus explained Himself in so many different ways and with so many different titles and examples, we can have certainty beyond a reasonable doubt that He really meant for us to treat Him as utterly unlike any leader or prophet who has ever lived. Be sure to draw out *why* members of your group responded the way they have.

Question 9 Outright rejection of Jesus would not necessarily be popular, so many people want to remake Jesus so He fits into their life without making demands on them. Any time we put words into Jesus' mouth that He didn't say—or take away words He did—we set ourselves up as superior to Him. Surely, one of the reasons Jesus said things in the radical way He did was so that we would wrestle with His claims and come to the truth instead of easily writing Him off and missing the point of His coming.

In an article called "Worshipping the Unknown God: The Heathen and Salvation," Greg Koukl notes, "This is why Jesus is so offensive. If you talk about God, everyone smiles and nods approval. Mention Jesus, though, and sparks fly. Jesus is God with a face, not the fill-in-the-blank variety we conform to our own tastes. He can't be twisted, distorted, and stuffed in our back pocket. That bothers people" (*Clear Thinking*, Fall 1995).

Session 3: Did Jesus Really Claim to Be God?

Short Answer: Though humbly living out His role as a servant, Jesus' teachings and actions made it clear He was both God and man.

Question 3 In order for an accurate picture of Jesus to emerge, we must see His full humanity as well as His deity. Modern people are more inclined to doubt His divine role (or to doubt His existence altogether), but there were also some in the early church who doubted Jesus' humanity. That is why, as early as the writings of the apostle John, it was pointed out that "Jesus Christ has come in the flesh" (1 John 4:1–3). This confusion about Jesus blossomed into a full-blown heresy called "docetism" and in the second century, "gnosticism." These people taught that God would not—and could not—condescend to take on humanity, so Jesus had just "appeared" (the Greek word is *dokeo*, hence *docetism*) to be a man. Their Jesus was only a spirit, a phantom who had no human birth, left no footprints as He walked, and did not really suffer on the cross.

Christian Science is a group today that embodies a similar mistaken view of Jesus. Christian Science teaches that the physical world is not real, and so Jesus did not have flesh because there is no such thing. It teaches that "the Christ" is separate from the man Jesus. The main thing for your group members to wrestle with here is that, whatever else we say about Jesus, He was fully human, just like us.

Question 4 The apostle John explained that he knew many stories about Jesus, but his reason for writing was so that "you may believe that Jesus is the Christ, the Son of God, and that by believing you may have life in his name" (John 20:30–31). The other gospel writers were also persuaded that Jesus was unlike any man who had ever lived. But rather than just claim that, they recorded the many unusual and miraculous things Jesus did, so that, for all of time, people could review the data for themselves and come to their own conclusions.

Question 6 Someone familiar with the Bible may point out that, at His trial, Jesus seemed to deny the charge of blasphemy by telling His accusers, "Well that's what you say (about me)" when they demanded He proclaim whether or not He was the Christ (Messiah), the Son of God. Some translations use the phrase, "You have said it yourself" or "You say that I am." That sounds to our ears like Jesus is denying the charge, or at least evading the question.

The reality is that Jesus was answering clearly in the affirmative. First, the phrase is not evasive, but an unequivocal statement of agreement. When Judas asked if he was the one who would betray Jesus, Jesus used the same phrase: "You have said

*Is Jesus
The Only
Way?*

23

it yourself" (Matthew 26:25). Was Jesus telling Judas he wasn't the betrayer? Second, the words following Jesus' answer at His trial make it unmistakably clear that He was claiming the role of Messiah. He quoted a passage from the book of Daniel in which "The Son of Man"—another messianic title—judges the whole world at the end of time. In effect, Jesus was saying, "Men, you may be my judges now, but a time is coming when you'll appear before Me in My heavenly court!" (see Mark 14:61–62). If Jesus had not been the Son of God, such a statement would have been blasphemous; it is the phrase that actually condemned Him. It is one of the strongest claims to Jesus' divinity in the Bible, and it comes straight out of His mouth. (Note: This information need not be brought up unless a group member asks.)

Question 8 To ignore Jesus or to relegate Him to a low-priority status would be unthinkable if He is really God's messenger to earth. Our lives simply cannot remain the same knowing that the great Creator of the universe has come among us to tell us of His love and His desire to forgive us and become leader of our lives.

Yet many people do that very thing. They are like the man C. S. Lewis described who ". . . is deliberately trying not to know whether Christianity is true or false, because he foresees endless trouble if it should turn out to be true. He is like the man who deliberately 'forgets' to look at the notice board because, if he did, he might find his name down for some unpleasant duty." Lewis continues, "You may not be certain yet whether you ought to be a Christian; but you do know you ought to be a man, not an ostrich, hiding its head in the sand" (*God in the Dark; Essays on Theology and Ethics*).

Your group members may feel bad that they haven't made Jesus a priority, or that their lives haven't lived up to His ideal. They may also be troubled by the narrowness of it all. One clear implication of God putting all of who He was in Jesus is that other truths, paths, and religions have more error in them than many have previously supposed. So although it's good news that we have a Savior in Jesus, it can trouble people to think about that ramification on their imperfect lives and on the lives of others who don't even care about Jesus.

Question 10 There is an intellectual side to this conclusion (the recognition of the *fact* of Jesus' deity) and an emotional side (the personal *embracing* of Him). The first says, "Jesus, You are the Lord" and the second says, "Jesus, You are *my* Lord." Of course,

Jesus is not content with convincing us of His role; He wants us to welcome and accept Him as the leader of our lives.

Session 4: Why Focus on Jesus' Death?

Short Answer: Jesus' mission was not finished until He died a sacrificial death for sin; Christians emphasize His death because He Himself did so—it was the culmination of everything He came to earth to do.

Question 2 In the spiritual realm, every sin rings up indebtedness—we take something away from God with each act of defiance. We exist, not because of any action on our part, but wholly because God, out of His great love, wanted to give us the experience of life. He owes us nothing; we owe Him everything. And each of our sins takes away some of the glory He is due as our creator.

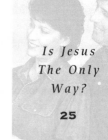
Picture each sin as the refusal to make a mortgage payment. If we stop sinning (repent) and start giving Him glory, that would be like starting to make mortgage payments after ceasing to do so. Yet we still owe for the times we didn't make the payments, even if we keep up with current amounts due. How will we make the past due payments? The Bible tells us the debt is too great and life is not long enough to ever pay in full— we just don't have it in us to give God what is His due and to make up for our offenses. That is why Christ's death, as a payment for us, is so precious: it releases us from ever having to worry that our spiritual mortgage will lapse. Jesus paid it all— not only past due amounts, *but the balance as well.* Spiritually speaking, there are no more payments due, *ever.* We are full owners of this thing called life, and the spiritual mansion we anticipate moving into in heaven is already ours because Christ paid the balance on the cross.

Question 4 Think of how we would view sin differently if every time we did something wrong, we were obligated to sacrifice a small animal to pay for that offense. Would we be as quick to go that route if we knew a death was the consequence? The irony is that every sin does create moral indebtedness with God—the pain of the animal is just a physical representation of that pain.

God clothing Adam and Eve shows His care for them. Clothing them with animal skins foreshadows what price is nec-

essary to make provision for their wrongdoing. It is interesting to note that when Adam wanted to make his own covering, he used fig leaves. Yet God's initiative required animal hides. This parallels human-made religion and God-ordained religion. Throughout the ages, people have tried to solve their spiritual problem using their own means—with results as humorous and ineffective as Adam's. God's means are more costly, but effective. And Christ's sacrifice was the most costly, and most effective, of all.

Question 5 The people of Israel would understand in the most powerful way that a covering of blood protected them from death. Spiritually, the covering of the blood of an innocent animal protects us from spiritual death. In the same way, the covering of Christ's blood covers us completely from eternal death. Note: Remember that some members of the group may not have Bibles with them so be sure to earmark the passage to be read in your own Bible before the meeting.

Questions 6 and 7 The people of Israel could do nothing except look at the serpent up on the pole and believe. There were no elaborate rituals, no self-help programs, no action on their part other than to respond in faith and trust God to do for them what they were unable to do for themselves.

Jesus was like that serpent, lifted up on a cross for all to see (John 3:14–15). We are all dying with the venom of sin. We can do nothing to save ourselves from its deadly poison; we must simply accept, on faith, that God can do it for us. It is not that there are lots of remedies and this is the best one—*there simply is no other cure.*

Question 8 Satan is the original kidnapper of the human race. Because he prevailed when he tempted Adam and Eve, they—and the rest of us—belong to him (1 John 5:19; Matthew 4:8–9; John 14:30; Ephesians 6:11–12). One intent of Jesus' death was to buy us back from the dominion of the evil one.

Question 11 A crossless Christianity is promise without fulfillment. It is hope for salvation from sin with no basis. It is God coming among us, but not willing to suffer for us. It is words without power. It is children who've been talked to for their wrongdoing, but not forgiven. It is a prophet, but no deliverer. In a crossless Christianity we are all still in our sins, looking at the One we sinned against eye-to-eye without any certainty of absolution.

Session 5: Isn't the Resurrection of Jesus a Myth?

Short Answer: No, it's a well-attested fact of history and foundational to the truth of Christianity.

General Note: Some critics of the resurrection have rightly observed that other religions have an idea of a rising god. Various fertility cults have a god that comes back to life each spring. The Egyptian god Osiris, husband of Isis also "resurrected." (Isis also had a son, Horus, who was "miraculously" conceived without a living father—claimed as yet another parallel to Christianity.) In the secular realm, Thomas Paine observed, "The story of Jesus Christ appearing after he was dead is the story of an apparition. . . . Stories of this kind had been told of the assassination of Julius Caesar." Because of these parallels, the uniqueness of Jesus' resurrection becomes suspect—as does the actual event itself.

Despite parallels, there are vast differences between Jesus' resurrection and these other myths or legends. The fertility gods resurrect annually; Jesus' resurrection was once and for all. Hearsay stories of other resurrections did not create a group of followers willing to die for those claims, but Jesus' disciples were prepared to do so—and all but one did. Besides, Jesus' followers were Jewish, and Jesus' resurrection blew apart their religious convention. The greatly renowned German New Testament scholar Joachim Jeremias calls attention to the fact that "Nowhere does one find in the [Jewish] literature anything comparable to the resurrection of Jesus. Certainly resurrections of the dead were known, but these always concerned resuscitations, the return to the earthly life. In no place in the late Judaic literature does it concern a resurrection to *doxa* (glory) as an event of history" (quoted by William Craig, "Contemporary Scholarship and the Historical Evidence for the Resurrection of Jesus Christ," posted on the Internet).

The fact that a rebirth idea is prevalent among various cultures may even be a "hard-wiring" in the human soul, put there by God so we would recognize Jesus (just as a conscience and God-awareness seem hard-wired into every person regardless of culture). So if the objection is raised that other religions have a rising god and therefore Jesus' resurrection is not unique, be ready to make your contribution to the discussion by pointing out that Jesus' resurrection is both categorically different and historically substantiated.

Question 9 A dead man rising is not your everyday occurrence, and it stretches the limits of what a rational person can accept. Actually, this is one of the reasons why God did it—so it would be spectacular beyond comparison, and would prove itself to be one of the all-time most dramatic miracles. As such, it's a beacon, a signal that something was going on in Jesus life that was totally unlike any other life in history.

Question 10 Group members may come up with a number of problems with the resurrection, but each probably stems from the highly unusual and statistically unlikely occurrence of a dead man coming back to life.

In spite of rational difficulties with the resurrection, if we grant that God is creator, then it really isn't such a stretch to imagine that the Giver of life and Creator of the cosmos can remake a dead corpse into a living being again. He who made the first man out of nonliving dirt can just as easily make the "last Adam" (1 Corinthians 15:45), Jesus, out of the remains left in the tomb. In the same way, God will remake all believers, regardless of the state of decay, into resurrected people to live with Him forever (Philippians 3:20–21).

Question 11 These points by Edwin M. Yamauchi might be helpful additional evidence: "Not even the most skeptical can deny the historical attestation of the faith of the early Christians in the Resurrection of Christ. This simple fact is of importance if we accept as genuine the numerous predictions of Jesus concerning his death and resurrection (Matt. 16:21; 17:9, 22,23; 20:18, 19; 26:2; etc.). Charlatans such as Theudas (Josephus, Antiquities XX. 5.1), who claimed to have the power to divide the Jordan River, or the Gnostic Menander, who claimed his disciples would remain ageless, were quickly exposed by the failure of their claims. The Qumran community, which has some features in common with the Christian community, did not survive the destruction of its monastery by the Romans in A.D. 68 because the people had no comparable faith to sustain them" ("Easter: Myth, Hallucination, or History?" posted on the Internet).

William Lane Craig perhaps best summarizes this subject when he writes, "Thus, none of the previous counter-explanations can account for the evidence as plausibly as the resurrection itself. One might ask, 'Well, then, how do skeptical scholars explain the facts of the resurrection appearances, the empty tomb, and the origin of the Christian faith?' The fact of the matter is, they don't. Modern scholarship recognizes no plausible explanatory alter-

native to the resurrection of Jesus. Those who refuse to accept the resurrection as a fact of history are simply self-confessedly left without an explanation.

"These three great facts—the resurrection appearances, the empty tomb, and the origin of the Christian faith—all point unavoidably to one conclusion: The resurrection of Jesus. Today the rational man can hardly be blamed if he believes that on that first Easter morning a divine miracle occurred" ("Contemporary Scholarship and the Historical Evidence for the Resurrection of Jesus Christ," posted on the Internet).

Session 6: What Difference Does Jesus Make Today?

Short Answer: Jesus' influence is in direct proportion to the access we grant Him into our lives and souls.

Question 1 It is almost always a fundamental misunderstanding about Jesus that causes people to do wrong things in His name. The problem isn't Jesus; it's the failure of His followers to truly follow Him consistently.

Question 3 Even if people don't follow Jesus, they are the beneficiaries of those in society who do (as noted in the Straight Talk "Imagine," just before this question).

Question 4 Here is one way to put Jesus' answers to life's biggest questions:

- Is there a God? Yes; and He wants to have first place in the hearts of His creatures.

- Why am I here? To live life to the full by being in a love relationship with God, first and foremost, and by loving my fellow creatures as well.

- Where am I ultimately going? God's desire is to share heaven with me forever.

Question 5 A life with Jesus boils down to loving others, not using them. It also calls us to put His kingdom first and to live by faith instead of frantically trying to accumulate the "stuff" of life and miss its real purpose.

Question 9 Your group members will come up with a variety of answers here, but based on the passages cited in Question 7, a fundamental difference most certainly would be a sense of peace and settledness. Life's circumstances would cease to be the indicators—or producers—of life's greatest happiness; rather, connection with God and conformity to His will would be paramount.

Question 10 Pay special attention to the responses you hear from the members of your group, as their answers could provide a great opportunity for you to engage in further conversation on an individual basis regarding their level of openness or readiness to becoming a Christian.

Question 11 Be sensitive to the possibility that this question could lead to a significant spiritual decision at this juncture. You may have a seeker in your group tell you he or she is actually ready at this point to receive Christ, or a lapsed believer may indicate readiness to "come home." Treat the moment reverently.

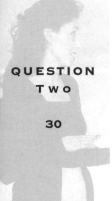

How Reliable Is the Bible?

Session 1: Where Did the Bible Come From?

Short Answer: The Bible was written by many people over many centuries.

Questions 3 and 4 Having the background and experience of people in the Bible helps make it a fully human book. It gives us the context so we can better understand its message. It tells us what humans thought and felt, which aids in our sense of connection with them and helps us relate to their clearly human actions and reactions. The fact that there is variety and yet consistency in spite of having many different authors gives the Bible greater credibility that God is behind its inspiration.

31

Question 6 The fact that the Bible was confirmed throughout a centuries-long process would safeguard against one person dominating the choices of which books to include or a faction imposing their theological bias. God's people, over time, *recognized* (and that's an important word; it wasn't a vote, *per se*, because the church can't *make* a work inspired) those books that came with divine authority and origin.

Question 7 When Christians centuries ago evaluated the books they received they used a three-fold test:

1. Did the book come from a prophet or apostle?

2. Did the book have doctrinal integrity—did it match revelation already accepted?

3. Did the book have wide acceptance—did many of God's people in several places validate these writings?

Such tests would probably preclude current books because

- the claim to prophetic status or apostolic authority could probably not be substantiated (Joseph Smith, the

Mormon prophet, fails the qualifications of a prophet because he gave some false predictions and taught things contrary to God's Word);

- the book would probably be at variance with some teaching in the Bible (books like the *Book of Mormon* or *Science and Health,* which claim to be from God, contradict biblical teaching);

- any contender today would have to be circulated among Christians all over the world in every culture and be received by all, which is not very likely.

Question 8 Because biblical prophets must be one hundred percent accurate, virtually all of today's so-called prophetic activity would be deemed spurious. In Old Testament days, prophets weren't likely to make such rash or careless predictions as those we see today, because death was the punishment for any incorrect statement following a "thus says the LORD." While capital punishment for false prophets is not appropriate in our day and age, rejection of the message and the messenger is a timeless biblical principle, and we would do well to follow it.

Question 9 Most people today are impressed by an unusual prediction, regardless of what else the person says. But some messages should be rejected no matter how "miraculous" the source (see Galatians 1:8). The Bible is clear that something unusual may not originate from God, and bad theology certainly doesn't. We need to be less impressed by what appears to be supernatural, and more discerning about the source—and what tags along with a message. To use a fishing analogy, we should be wary of swallowing a dangerous theological or pseudo-spiritual "hook" when we bite the "worm" of a supposedly miraculous event or prediction.

Session 2: Isn't the Bible Full of Myths?

Short Answer: No, not in the sense of stories that claim to be authentic but are actually fictional. The Bible contains many made-up stories, but those are clearly identified as such.

Question 3 Many allege that the Bible contains all three kinds of myths mentioned in the Straight Talk preceding this question. The most scandalous myths, however, are those in which

religious dogma is put forth as real and necessary to believe, but for which there is little historical or rational support. Those who contend the Bible includes this type of myth would describe that part of the Bible as sort of a "pious fraud," where a writer thought something would help others even if he knew it wasn't true. Also, people might say the storyteller thought the material was something God wanted him to write, so he went ahead, hoping for some divine reward, even though he knew he was making it up. Another possible motive for fraud is the writer's hope for power or prestige that would follow publication.

Question 4 Most stories in the Bible that are parables or fiction are introduced with verbal clues to their nature. Examples include such statements as "*suppose* a man had two sons . . ." and "I will tell you what heaven *is like.* . . ." Historical material, on the other hand, omits such disclaimers and has lots of detail typical of eyewitness accounts.

Question 5 People may just be gullible by nature, and so they accept the Bible—a good thing—for bad reasons. If these people had been in another culture, they may have accepted the wrong things with the same uncritical approval. God doesn't commend gullibility. If you or your group members' foundation for truth is shaky, it's never too late to get good reasons for good beliefs.

Question 6 Most critics are surprisingly emotional when it comes to their criticism of the Bible's miraculous elements. We who believe would do well to listen better as we relate to these people. It can help immensely to learn *how* such a critical attitude developed. Most likely, the person was forced to accept things at an early age without question and was never encouraged to test the reliability or reasonableness of the belief system presented to them. That can leave a bitter taste in a person's mouth when it comes to spiritual truth. You may want to use this question to address some of your group members' issues regarding their skeptical stance toward the Bible.

Question 7 If a worldwide event such as the flood in Noah's time truly happened, one would expect there would be many stories concerning that event in various cultures. "The Flood is told of by the Greeks, the Hindus, the Chinese, the Mexicans, the Algonquins, and the Hawaiians. Also, one list of Sumerian kings treats the Flood as a real event" (Norman Geisler and Ron Brooks, *When Skeptics Ask*). The presence of numerous accounts distributed among many peoples increases the historic probability that the event described actually occurred, even if the accounts vary somewhat.

Question 10 Books on archaeology and comparative studies in other literature similar to the Bible would be a great place to start reading. Another thing to do might be to talk to others who do trust the Bible and find out why they believe in it.

Session 3: What About All Those Contradictions?

Short Answer: The claim of contradictions in the Bible is grossly exaggerated, and what problems that do exist can be harmonized.

Questions 3 and 4 These questions (and the information in the accompanying Straight Talk "Contradictions and the Character of God") form sort of a test case for how to resolve an alleged contradiction in the Bible. Sometimes, it's as easy as just taking the effort to understand the context, point of view, or intent of the different writers. At the same time, we have to be open to new ways to understand familiar concepts (in the example, we need to broaden our concept of God, not accuse the writers of contradicting each other). When we do this, we can see that the Bible is in harmony with itself.

Questions 5 and 6 If one of the cross inscriptions read "Rudolph the Red-Nosed Reindeer," *then* we'd have a contradiction! The variations shown in the Straight Talk "Contradictions and the Cross" reveal *partial* information recorded in each Gospel, but not *contradictory* information. Also, the fact that there were three inscriptions in different languages could account for some of the variations; if the inscriptions were slightly different in the different languages, one gospel writer could have recorded only what one language said, and other writers could have recorded the other, slightly differently worded inscription.

Question 7 By leaving the apparent contradictions, the copyists show there was no attempt to collude or artificially correct the text. They believed it was better to be accurate and preserve manuscript integrity than to harmonize.

Question 8 Human beings are prone to misunderstanding, simply because we are finite. Nothing is beyond potential confusion as long as we're human. That doesn't mean we can't have *substantial* understanding, but it does mean that there's noth-

ing God could do, short of granting us omniscience, to eliminate all possible error in our thinking.

Take, for example, the simple sign, "No Parking After 2-
Inch Snow Fall." Patrick C. Heston, in his tongue-in-cheek article "Theology of a City Street Sign" (*The Wittenburg Door*),
points out the many ways this sign could be understood—or
misunderstood:

- Is it a command ("don't do it") or a description ("try
  as you may, you won't be able to")?

- Is it literal snow or could it allude to figurative elements
  including cocaine or heroin?

- The sign doesn't say where the snow must fall—what
  if it's in the next county?

- Does the snow have to fall all at once, or could two or
  three snowfalls accumulate past two inches?

- What if some of the snow fell before midnight, and the
  rest after?

- What if it's a 1.9-inch snowfall?

- What if it snows more than two inches—is it limited to
  snowfalls of exactly two inches, no more, no less?

- What if it snows two inches, but doesn't stick?

- Does it mean the first snowfall of two inches after the
  sign goes up, or every one after that?

- Does it mean cars only, or include trucks? What about
  boats?

- Does the sign prohibit parking everywhere in the city
  after snow, or just the streets?

- If you've already parked before the snow falls, can you
  stay parked, because technically, you're not parking *after*
  the two inch snow fall?

- Does it mean "after" in the sense of "in the manner
  of"—so you can't park *the way* snow falls?

- How soon after the snow falls can you park again?

Clearly, any simple statement can be disputed—and especially one which is complicated or abstract. That's why we need
to follow good principles of interpretation. The amazing thing

about the Bible is how much is agreed upon in spite of the many ways its message could be understood.

Session 4: Hasn't the Bible Changed Over Time?

Short answer: No, the ancient manuscripts we now have assure us that current translations are extremely close to the original text.

Question 3 Because the copies we have are dated so early, although the originals are lost, there is certainty about virtually 99.9% of the Bible. And no questionable verse is the basis for any doctrine.

Questions 4 and 5 The wide distribution of biblical texts is a safeguard against corruption because there are so many manuscripts to compare. Nothing in all of ancient literature even comes close to the massive amount of manuscript evidence for the New Testament.

Questions 7 and 8 The fact that nonbiblical sources and archaeological discoveries support various details about biblical history helps us see with even more certainty that the Bible writers were concerned with accurate history, not just with writing a biased "sales brochure" for Christianity.

Another great example of archaeological confirmation is the prophecy about the city of Tyre (Ezekiel 26). After thirteen years of being seiged, in 572 B.C. the city of Tyre made terms with the most powerful army in the world, the Babylonians. The city's name meant *rock*, and, after holding out against Nebuchadnezzar, it retained its island stronghold, though the mainland part of the city was destroyed. Despite its reputation as an impregnable fortress ("The Rock"), the Bible predicted the future destruction of Tyre: "They will break down your walls and demolish your fine houses and throw your stones, timber and rubble into the sea" (Ezekiel 26:12, dated around 570 B.C. by most scholars). Adding to the odds against this prediction was the fact that most Middle East cities, once destroyed, were rebuilt on the same site after covering the ruins with soil. Despite these facts, this prophecy was literally fulfilled in 332 B.C. by Alexander the Great. After demolishing the city, he cast all of the debris (right down to the bare rock—especially ironic in light of the meaning of the word "Tyre") into the sea to create a giant land bridge out to the island stronghold. This bridge still exists today and contains the ruins of Tyre—exactly as predicted.

Question 10 Of course, someone who just doesn't *want* to believe can't be convinced to do so. "No one *will* believe unless they are *willing* to believe" (Peter Kreeft and Ronald K. Tacelli, *Handbook of Christian Apologetics*). The only way to help such a person is to find out the real reason behind their resistance. Until that is identified, talking about other evidence is a waste of time. The discussion questions in this guide are designed to do just that—to assist you in helping your group members uncover real reasons for their own resistance, past or present. Even in Jesus' day, people saw Him do miracles but didn't believe in Him. For some, their hardness of heart kept them from belief, despite their recognition that He was extraordinary.

Session 5: Why Should I Trust the Bible?

Short Answer: The Bible can be trusted because it is accurate, it bears evidence of divine authorship, and it was endorsed by Jesus, the most trustworthy person in history.

Question 2 Some people think that if Jesus had written his own book, we could have a more complete picture. Yet that is not necessarily the case. Autobiographies are not inherently more comprehensive or accurate—possibly, quite the contrary. Four writers rather than just one give us a fuller perspective, guarding against bias or failure to include the most relevant details.

Question 3 Most people are surprised to see statements like the first few verses to Luke's gospel, because the popular assumption is that history doesn't matter in the realm of religion. Yet Christianity is one of the few religions not based on a philosophy but rooted in historic events. If these events did not occur, whatever else it teaches is of little or no value.

Question 5 Clearly, Peter, John, and Paul knew the difference between true events and "cleverly invented stories." They were giving their lives for things they saw and events they lived through. They knew mixing falsehood or exaggerations would damage their credibility. Considering the amount of persecution they endured, it was no small thing to be sure that what they were teaching was real.

Question 9 A myth can have a powerful affect on a person, as can a deliberate lie. The "change factor" of the Bible has limits with respect to how much it establishes the Bible's credibility. Muslims would say the Quran has changed their lives; does that mean it has to be God's Word? However, once a person sees the Bible has credibility on other levels, its good to know it is not only right, but it also *works*.

Session 6: Is the Bible Really God's Book?

Short Answer: More than any other book in the world, the Bible has the stamp of divine involvement.

Question 2 What comes from God must not just be true, but must have power. Obviously, those writings must claim to be from God. The Bible is reliable, both historically and in terms of how its principles make a difference. As former president Calvin Coolidge said, "In this Book [the Bible] will be found the solution of all the problems of the world." (cited in *The Complete Book of Practical Proverbs and Wacky Wit*, by Vern McLellan).

Question 4 One might argue that psychics sometimes predict things that eventually come true. Does that make them from God? There are vast differences between Bible prophecy and so-called psychics. For one, Bible predictions came true centuries later. For another, Bible prophecies were very specific, unlike those who say something like, "Good fortune is coming your way." Finally, the Bible writers exalt God with accurate teaching about Him, whereas psychics tend to exalt themselves and make money off the gullible public.

Question 6 We think the strongest argument for the Bible's divine inspiration is the unconditional support it got from Jesus when He was here. Geisler and Brooks include the following chart in their book *When Skeptics Ask:*

What Jesus Taught About the Old Testament

1. Authority—Matthew 22:43

2. Reliability—Matthew 26:54

3. Finality—Matthew 4:4,7,10

4. Sufficiency—Luke 16:31

5. Indestructibility—Matthew 5:17–18

6. Unity—Luke 24:27,44

7. Clarity—Luke 24:27

8. Historicity—Matthew 12:40

9. Facticity (scientifically)—Matthew 19:2–5

10. Inerrancy—Matthew 22:29; John 3:12; 17:17

11. Infallibility—John 10:35

Anyone holding to an inferior position about Scripture must, in effect, contend with Jesus—not theologians—on this matter.

Question 9 Prayer is powerful, but prayer doesn't tell you if the Bible is God's Word. (Presumably, it's the *answer* to that prayer that would do that!) The Bible doesn't ever tell a person to use an answer to prayer as a way to sort out truth and error; we are all too prone to subjective influences to make this our final authority. As noted in the introduction to *How Reliable is the Bible?* (see pp. 9–10), such methodology wouldn't help you distinguish between the Bible and other contenders with sufficient certainty to base your life on it. We need hard data along with more subjective input.

Question 10 The implications of the Bible's message have scared away many people from accepting it. Like Mark Twain, they see what it's demanding and they don't want to give in to those demands. They see that they will need to give an account to the God of the universe, and that may scare them.

As far as acceptance, sometimes people just read the Bible and like it, and so for that simple reason, they come to trust it. That's not bad, but it may not be enough to withstand future times of testing. Therefore, for those who come to belief easy, it's probably a good idea to fortify that foundation with more research into why the Bible is worth trusting.

How Could God Allow Suffering and Evil?

Session 1: Where Did Evil Come From?

Short Answer: God did not create evil; evil entered the world as the consequence for sin after humankind's rebellion against God.

Question 1 This question is designed to be an icebreaker for your group to discuss various encounters with hardship. People may have different definitions of what is meant by the word "evil" but don't let that distract your group from discussing various situations that have caused them to wonder why these sorts of things happen. After sharing openly about some of the difficulties faced in their lives, your group members will be better prepared to discuss the topic of this session.

Question 2 An interesting side note is pointed out by Peter Kreeft and Ronald K. Tacelli in their book *Handbook of Christian Apologetics*: "The fact that we do not naturally accept this world full of injustice, suffering, sin, disease and death—the very fact of our outrage at evil is a clue that we are in touch with a standard of goodness by which we judge this world as defective, as falling drastically short of the mark. The fact that we judge something evil might even be developed into an argument for the existence of the standard of Perfect Goodness implied in our judgment, and thus for the existence of the God of perfect goodness whom evil's existence seems to disprove."

Question 3 Most people feel that moral evil is the direct result of bad choices made by other humans and that natural evil is something from God. Therefore they tend to blame people for moral evil, and God for natural evil. (Actually, they blame God for not preventing moral evil, so He gets blame either way!) The reality is that both kinds of evil have their source in people, because natural evil wouldn't have ever happened if mankind hadn't sinned. Therefore, the more accurate picture is that humankind is responsible for both moral and natural evil, though group members need not come to that conclusion this early in the session.

Question 5 This question invites group members to express their frustrations with how much evil there is in the world and allows them to conclude that God may not even exist at all—or at least not in the form the Bible claims. Do not feel the pressure to refute this point of view, since other possible conclusions regarding the problem of evil will be presented later in the session.

Question 6 Because God knew there was a risk that people would use their freedom to reject Him (and, as a result, bring evil into the world), we can infer that God places a very high value on freedom of choice. Given the extent of evil in our world, He must think freedom of choice is *extremely* valuable indeed. Knowing that Jesus died to bring us back to God also indicates how precious the freedom to choose is. Clearly, an authentic, noncoercive relationship between God and people is one of the most valuable things in the world.

Question 7 Humankind sinned, which produced an immediate separation from God. Evil and suffering were a direct result. After our rebellion, "all hell broke loose"—literally. The evil around us is both the consequence of our rebellion and a taste of what is to come for those who want a world where God is entirely absent. (The Bible calls that world hell.)

Question 8 Some people in your group may agree with this statement because exercising free will by definition means that people are not programmed to always choose God. Others in your group may disagree, saying that God could have given us free will and at the same time put in us a compelling desire to want only what is good.

Question 9 This question is asking if the freedom to choose is something your group members value, or if would they prefer a robot-like existence. We think most people will see the value in being human and free rather than being mere automatons. Since that is how an all-wise God created us, it seems consistent with His view and the better of the two options.

Question 11 It is perfectly natural to feel anger toward God when we don't understand life. The Bible is full of examples in which people openly and honestly brought out their confu-

sion and vented at God. The Psalms, inspired by the Holy Spirit, are full of such lament. This question can give you the opportunity to help your group members see that it is appropriate to take their problems and feelings and bring them right out in the open before God. He is willing and able to handle their concerns, even when they are presented "imperfectly."

Session 2: Why Doesn't God Do Something?

Short Answer: He *has* done something through Jesus Christ; this act must hold us over until, at the end of time, He rights every wrong.

Question 1 Use this question to allow group members to open up to each other about their lives. Doing so will build bridges of trust and support for one another. Be sure to encourage the personal side of the group experience. A small group is not just a "class" but rather an opportunity for life-change to occur.

Question 3 You may want to point out the fact that the Bible itself doesn't ignore these kinds of tough questions. Habakkuk wondered about the same perplexing issues we face today. Writer Dorthy Sayers reminds us that God took suffering upon Himself as well: "For whatever reason God chose to make man as he is— limited and suffering and subject to sorrows and death—He had the honesty and courage to take His own medicine. Whatever game He is playing with His creation, He has kept His own rules and played fair. He can exact nothing from man that He has not exacted from Himself. He has Himself gone through the whole of human experience, from the trivial irritations of family life and the cramping restrictions of hard work and lack of money, to the worst horrors of pain and humiliation, defeat, and death. When He was a man, He played the man. He was born in poverty and He died in disgrace and thought it well worthwhile."

Question 5 The implication is that all of us would be wiped out in such a sweeping removal of evil.

Question 7 Group members may suggest that one possible option would be for God to give us the freedom to choose but limit our choices to only good ones; that, however, is an impossibility because it is a contradiction in terms—there is no real choice if there is no real possibility for the opposite to occur.

Question 8 God seems to be patiently waiting for all of us to take advantage of the opportunity to choose Him. He tolerates evil for the sake of those who've not yet come to Him, which means His patience with evil is not some sort of weakness or indecision but a gracious act of compassion toward those who've not yet repented.

Question 9 By allowing people to experience evil firsthand, we are exposed a little bit to what life is like without God. Once we've seen this, we can make a more educated choice about what it is we really want. Although it is conjecture, perhaps the whole universe is learning a lesson through humanity's failure that could serve worlds and beings yet to be created!

Question 10 Even knowing that evil may someday be wiped out doesn't necessarily reduce the pain and suffering being experienced now.

Session 3: Why Do Innocent People Suffer?

Short Answer: In one sense, there are no truly innocent people, so no truly innocent people suffer; yet it is in the very nature of evil that it does not discriminate among its victims, which is why it is so volatile and dangerous (and why God is so opposed to our committing more evil).

Question 5 God set natural laws in place and doesn't interfere as they take their course. When sin entered the picture, those natural laws continued to operate, but with some distortion. Disasters are not caused by some sort of meddling by God; rather, disasters are due to this mutilation of nature.

Question 6 We often react to pain with the knee-jerk reaction of blame, even if we're the ones who are responsible. Often God is the One we get mad at, despite the reality that He may have had nothing at all to do with the problem.

Question 7 The presence of someone else's pain doesn't obligate us to help, at least not in the sense that people are exempt from taking responsibility for their own choices. Yet because we who are followers of a compassionate Savior are commanded to help others, we have a duty to care based on Christ's example and request. There are times when the most loving thing to do is let someone feel the effects of a sinful choice (as when an alcoholic is allowed to lose the enabling behavior of a spouse). But for the believer, the act is always one of compassion, even if pain results.

Question 8 God's guidelines given to us in the Bible are designed to keep us from hurting God, others, or ourselves. His blueprint for living is not a way to keep us from enjoying life but instead leads to life without regrets or unneeded pain.

Question 9 The point C. S. Lewis is making is that, based on the choices we have made to reject God, it seems consistent that we ought to be experiencing more suffering and evil than we do. It is only by God's goodness and grace that we have not already received what is justly due for the sins we've committed. God has put at work in the world a restraining power that is buffering the effects of evil (2 Thessalonians 2:7). Were that restraint removed, we would have true hell on earth. In his book *The Goodness of God*, John Wenham adds, "Because sin deserves death and we are all sinners, it means that all our mercies are undeserved mercies. Any apparent unfairness in God's treatment of us arises not because some have too much punishment, but because some of us appear to have too little. None of us will ever receive harsher judgment than we ever deserve . . . The marvel is, in the biblical view, not that men die for their sins, but that we remain alive in spite of them."

Question 10 In case some members of your group have difficulty coming up with positive results for suffering, be prepared to give an example from your own life.

Question 12 You may want to point out that the alternatives suggested by the members of your group may not capture our attention in quite the same way that pain and suffering would. If pain is not strong enough, we will just ignore it. Without the sensation of pain, a child might be tempted to touch the flames of a fire without reflexively pulling away—resulting in irreparable destruction of tissue. In that sense, pain is a gift to keep us from actions that destroy the body. Likewise, guilt can be a gift that urges us to stop other destructive behavior.

Session 4: Is the Devil for Real?

Short Answer: Yes, he is a fallen angel in rebellion against God and seeks to gather other people into his web of defiance.

Question 2 Hopefully, group members will see the relevancy of discussing this topic. Determining the reality of an evil spiritual being raises the awareness level needed to take the devil seriously, which, in turn, enables effective use of countermeasures.

Question 3 Because of the credibility of Jesus argued in the previous session, His statements about the devil should be taken seriously. In some ways, knowing Jesus believed in the devil ends the discussion, because if Jesus is the trustworthy Son of God, would *you* want to accuse Him of error?

Question 4 The devil wanted Jesus to listen to him and obey him. The devil tempted Him to submit to his challenges, but Jesus resisted him by quoting God's Word back to him.

Question 5 The devil took the words of God and twisted and distorted them in an attempt to confuse and deceive Eve. God hadn't said they couldn't touch the tree; Satan added that to make God's request seem unreasonable. He also called God a liar and painted a picture of a stingy, overbearing God. Satan's temptation was not ultimately about the fruit; it was about getting Eve to accept a distorted picture of God. That was Satan's ultimate aim, and it remains his goal to this day. R. C. Sproul says, "Satan is described as an accuser, a liar, and a tempter. We see him lying, distorting the truth, we see him involved in temptation, and we see him accusing the saints" (*Now, That's a Good Question!*).

Question 6 Misery loves company! The very fact that the devil has rejected God means he would enjoy seeing others share in that rejection. (He is happy to allow this rejection of God to masquerade as neutrality toward God).

Question 7 For reasons not totally clear, God has allowed Satan a certain amount of freedom to cause trouble here on earth. Some of the evil and suffering we experience is a direct result of Satan's attacks on us.

Question 8 The Bible does not give a clear answer to this question. It seems that God is waiting to bring judgment to Satan and the world at a later time.

Question 9 Even though God has allowed the devil to exercise power on this earth, God has limited that power and remains in ultimate control.

Session 5: How Could a Loving God Send People to Hell?

Short Answer: He doesn't; people send themselves to hell by ignoring the One willing to receive and forgive. A loving God is doing everything He can to get people to stop their stubborn resistance.

Questions 2, 3, and 4 People who examine the source of their belief about hell may discover they have inadequate reasons for their views. This discovery may spur them on to getting a better foundation for what they believe about such an important topic—especially seeing as the subject has eternal ramifications!

Question 5 Ultimately, the reason people wind up in hell is not because God sent them there, but because people prefer hell to submission to God. Hell is the ultimate separation from God. It is the eternal destiny that logically follows a lifetime of choosing to omit God from one's life. Jesus wept over Jerusalem, wanting—longing—to gather the inhabitants to Himself, but like so many others throughout time, *they were unwilling.*

Question 6 The Bible seems to be teaching that hell is a literal and actual place. The torments are emotional (regret), spiritual (separation from God), and perhaps even physical (burning). Whatever the specifics, hell is an utterly undesirable place described in the Bible with a variety of negative analogies.

Question 8 Cliffe Knechtle addresses this issue in his book *Give Me an Answer*: "God is not merely a doddering old grandfather with a white beard who sits on a throne in the sky and smiles as he lets everyone pass by. He's not hanging around saying, 'Well, Hitler, you murdered a few folks at Dachau, Buchenwald and Auschwitz, but I understand you're simply a product of your environment. I'm all-forgiving; enter heaven.' That's not being loving—that's amoral. Instead of asking, 'How could a caring God allow a hell to exist?' the question ought to be, 'How could a caring God not allow a hell to exist?'"

Question 9 The existence of hell can be a kind of good news, especially to those who suffered at the hands of others. It's the place where God tells the victim of sexual abuse, "I will confine your abuser here so he can't hurt you any more"; where He tells all those who've suffered under oppression, "Those who didn't see you as human won't be allowed to have any sway anymore"; where all moral pollution is contained so that none of us have to suffer the consequences of those who refuse to give up their evil ways.

Question 10 People do not usually realize that resisting God is actually distancing themselves from Him, which is a foretaste of the ultimate separation from God found in hell. We trivialize our resistance to God, thinking that we have a better way (which is why we resist God). The reality is that God's ways are always best, even though, in the short run, we don't always see why.

Question 11 Hell is God's way of preserving human dignity. He recognizes and honors the right of people to choose, including the choice to reject a relationship with Him. His justice is shown not in overlooking sin, but causing it to have consequences. His love is shown in sending His Son as payment for sin, which provides a choice for mankind to come back to God. It is also because of God's love that He has warned us about the destination awaiting those who continue to live distanced from God.

Session 6: Is There Really a Heaven?

Short Answer: Yes, and we have the awesome privilege of enjoying its beauty and splendor if we choose to let God forgive us so we can go there.

Question 4 Jesus' words about heaven assure us of at least two things: first, it must exist if an authority of the stature of Jesus says so; second, if He is preparing a place for us, it must be a wonderful and personal place, because someone of Jesus' power and love is behind its creation and adaptation for us.

Question 5 The point of this question is to expose people's expectations of what they think it takes to enter heaven. The standard that God has set for people to enter heaven is perfection. That standard is too high for anyone to measure up, which means no one can enter heaven based on good deeds alone. Unless you have a perfect record, forgiveness is required to get into heaven.

Question 6 Sinful people gain entrance into heaven because of the payment Jesus made when He died for our sins. When a person places his faith and trust in what Christ has done in paying that penalty, he can be absolutely confident that he is

restored into a relationship with God and will enter heaven in the hereafter.

Question 7 This question provides a great opportunity for you to discover where the members of your group are spiritually. Use it as a chance to help people see their need to accept Jesus Christ into their lives. For those who have received salvation but are doubting, remind them that, if they have trusted Christ, their entering heaven is now a matter of Christ's trustworthiness, not based on anything they can do. They can have confidence in their destination based on the promises of God (1 John 5:11–13).

Questions 9 and 10 Although thinking about heaven has been criticized as diverting one's attention from critical matters at hand on earth, confidence in heaven can lead to a peace and calmness that can be a great blessing. Knowing your future is settled can help you serve with greater freedom, and knowing there's a better day ahead can keep you going when the going gets tough.

Don't All Religions Lead to God?

Session 1: Don't All Religions Teach Basically the Same Thing?

Short Answer: No. After careful examination, major differences of doctrine and practice will be discovered, especially as compared with Christianity.

Question 2 Many of your group members will probably comment that the major religions are basically the same. Their reasons might include things like: all religions promote goodwill toward others and God. At this point, accept everybody's comments; don't be tempted to argue against this way of thinking.

Question 3 The reasoning behind this question is to raise the issue that even though a religion might be inspiring people to live their lives—*which is a good thing*—it might not contain the truth about how to find a relationship with God. The religion may very well only improve some aspect of life now, without providing for eternity—which would be a terrible tragedy. As Greg Koukl concludes, "If issues of religion have eternal consequences, then errors in thinking are infinitely tragic. To rephrase Karl Marx, false religion is the opiate of the people. It soothes, but does not cure" (*Clear Thinking*, Summer 1996).

Question 5 There are times when people do claim, in an arrogant and conceited way, to have the truth about religion. This attitude probably exists with some members of all religions but it wouldn't be reason enough to necessarily discredit that religion. A person's arrogance can, however, cause others to be less open to that particular religion.

Question 6 It may seem humble—and even logical—that each of us in the world have a small piece of the total truth, and that is what explains all the different religions in the world. That

51

analogy breaks down, however, when you consider the poem regarding the blind men and the elephant. In it, the men are all groping for the truth, yet finding only pieces of it. But if the elephant could talk and reveal what he was like to the blind men, they would have the total picture. Christianity is not blind men reaching for God (as is the case with man-made religions); it is God coming to blind men to clearly explain Himself in Christ. In Christianity, the elephant tells us what he's like.

Question 8 The idea that we should accept all religions in spite of differences is a very popular view called pluralism. The problem with this way of thinking is that it defies logic and reasoning. Two things that contradict each other cannot both be true at the same time. Tolerance, which says we should accept people even if we reject ideas, is commendable; but pluralism, which says everyone is right, is impossible and dishonest. Grantley Morris adds, "To overlook obvious differences between religions might seem broad-minded. In reality it is about as proud and narrow as a person could get. To say all religions are basically the same is to claim to be smarter than each of the billions of people who believe the unique aspects of their religion are of supreme importance to God. It is to claim that even though you are an expert in their religion you know they are wrong—you know their religion is really no different. Jesus made Godlike claims of this scale but he backed them up by living a perfect life, walking on water, calming a storm, multiplying bread and fish, healing people born blind or deaf or crippled, rising bodily from the dead, dramatically changing the lives of believers for 2,000 years, and so on. Your decision about religion is as serious as a starving person deciding whether to risk eating something which might be deadly. To most people, wild mushrooms are all much the same and who cares anyhow? But when there is nothing else to eat, it becomes rather important whether the type you choose is poisonous. And if you eat nothing for weeks, not making a decision becomes as deadly as the worse decision" (Posted on the Internet).

Question 9 The significant difference between these two statements is the credibility of the one promoting the belief. In the first statement, personal opinion is the proof; in the second, the authority is Jesus Christ himself, not the one who holds the belief. (Note: The credibility of Jesus was discussed in the another guide in this series, *Is Jesus the Only Way.*)

Question 10 Tolerance promotes the freedom to believe whatever a person wants to believe. Validation of a religion promotes the acceptance of that religion as truth, or valid.

Question 11 Christianity doesn't say that every religion has *only* falsehood; it teaches that although some truth may be found there, no other religion began with God's initiative and has enough truth to save those depending on it.

Question 12 It may be frustrating to some members of your group that God would allow so many different religions. The question might be raised: Why doesn't God narrow down the choices so it's easier to find Him? To do that, God would have to step in and take away our freedom of choice, which the Bible tells us He is not about to do. So He allows false religion, even as He allows other poor choices of people. In the midst of the confusion stands the teaching and work of Jesus, a shining light in the darkness. His lighthouse is showing the way, even though many ignore it.

Question 14 It is possible for Christianity to be true and for a Christian to be accepting toward others who believe differently. We can still love the person, even with his or her imperfections and wrong ideas (as we are loved with all our imperfections and wrong ideas). Jesus Himself taught about humility and accepting others. He also taught that it is through love that we are to help people see the truth.

Session 2: Isn't It Enough to Be Sincere?

Short Answer: No. It is possible to be sincerely wrong; therefore, it is important to be both sincere and right.

Question 1 This question is designed to expose the frustration most people have about insincerity, especially insincerity within religion. While insincerity within religious beliefs is not a good thing, neither is sincerity within falsehood. The goal is to help people see the need to be sincere *and* correct.

Question 3 This question hits at the popular view that no matter what people believe, it is okay as long as they are sincere. By the end of this session, group members should get the idea that this way of thinking can not logically be right.

Question 4 One advantage would be the simplicity of the system. But it would lead to great harm in almost every area of life, because truth—*reality*—would no longer matter. The world would become a nightmare, with every action justified by sincerity. In addition, how much sincerity is necessary? Is anyone *totally* sincere? Aren't we all a mixed bag? Also, a God of justice would be a joke; there would be no justice, only sincerity.

Question 5 Both sincerity and actions matter. One without the other leads to problems.

Question 6 A person's sincere belief, one way or the other, does not effect the essence of the truth of something. An apple is a fruit. One person may eat it and another person may not. But the apple does not stop being a fruit just because someone didn't eat it. Abraham Lincoln once quipped, "Suppose you call a tail a leg. How many legs does a dog have? The answer is four; calling a tail a leg doesn't make it one."

Question 7 Sincerity makes error into a tragedy, not a truth.

Question 8 Cliffe Knechtle states, "Truth matters when you go take a test. The day of judgment will be the final exam when you and I will stand before God and have to give an account for all of our actions, all of our words, all of our thoughts. And the question is, are you ready for that final exam" (*Give Me an Answer*). For some reason, many people understand that it is possible to be sincerely wrong in a wide variety of situations in our world, but when it comes to religion and God, the popular opinion is that sincerity matters more than what might really be right. This is tragic, because it leads to complacency and misses the entire purpose of life: to live with God and enjoy Him both now and forever.

Session 3: What's So Different About Christianity?

Short Answer: Christianity is the only religion that teaches salvation is a gift from God offered through Jesus Christ, not something a person can earn by following a set of religious guidelines.

Question 3 It would seem that the credibility of both the scripture and the founder should matter a great deal. It is interesting that many followers of religions do not make this a priority for validating what they devote themselves to. Often more superficial factors such as social convention, benefits derived from membership in the group, subjective experiences and feelings when in the group, and current leadership (a real nice guy in charge of the local assembly), are more convincing.

Question 5 Each of these four major world religions may have some truth to them, but when they are promoting teachings that logically contradict each other, they cannot all be the truth. They describe radically different Gods (or no God at all), radically different ways to connect with God (or find ultimate meaning), and radically different lifestyles that reflect God's character.

Question 6 All four of these religions teach that salvation is obtained through a process of performing certain duties. In all these schemes, salvation is earned, not a free gift.

Question 7 There is always an element of ambiguity with such systems: "Have I done enough? Was my wrong too wrong?" You never know where you stand. This uncertainty leaves people frustrated and fearful.

Question 8 The thing that sets Christianity apart from all other religions is that Christianity clearly states salvation is a gift, not something that can be earned. C. S. Lewis points out that Christianity's founder, Jesus Christ, is the only religious leader who made claims to deity: "There is no half-way house, and there is no parallel in other religions. If you had gone to Budda and asked, 'Are you the son of Bramah?' he would have said, 'You are still in a veil of illusion.' If you had gone to Socrates and asked, 'Are you Zeus?' he would have laughed at you. If you had gone to Mohammed and asked, 'Are you Allah? He would first have rent his clothes and then cut your head off. If you asked Confucius, 'Are you heaven? I think he probably would have replied: 'Remarks which are not in accordance with nature are in bad taste.' The idea of a great moral teacher saying what Christ said is out of the question. In my opinion, the only person who can say that sort of thing is either God or a complete lunatic suffering from that form of delusion which undermines the whole mind of man..." (*God in the Dark*).

Question 9 It is amazing to think that people would believe in reincarnation when there is no evidence for it. Even if you put forward supposed past-life regressions and memories of those lives, reincarnation teaches that we come back as animals and inanimate objects—where's the evidence for that? Much is at stake here because without reincarnation Buddhism and Hinduism cannot stand.

Question 12 Many people feel that one's religion is not necessarily something they choose for themselves, but that the culture in which they are raised determines what they believe. While that may experientially true, it is not a good way to proceed with such an important decision. People may become entrenched in their belief systems because change is uncomfortable. It's a frightening thing to face one's errors—who enjoys admitting we've been wrong? Yet we all need to know why we believe whatever we believe. God holds us accountable for the light we've been given and what we've done with it.

Session 4: Aren't Mormons and Jehovah's Witnesses Christians Too?

Short Answer: No. The teachings of both Mormons and Jehovah's Witnesses are not consistent with historic, biblical Christianity on major points of belief and practice, despite some similarities.

Question 2 It's important to humanize members of these faiths. They are people just like you and me who've gotten caught in a theological system of half-truths and error.

Question 3 This will help you as the leader to know how familiar your group members are with these groups. In *So What's the Difference?* Fritz Ridenour has the following to say about the Jehovah's Witnesses: "Jehovah's Witnesses are a challenge to Christians for several reasons: (1) Most of their growth has taken place just recently; (2) they will probably continue growing because they preach their message to a world on the brink of nuclear war; (3) their teachings are flatly opposed to the gospel; (4) they are flatly opposed to the Christian church which they say is of the devil; (5) they deny the deity of Jesus Christ, the person and work of the Holy Spirit and many other vital doctrines; and (6) they claim that their teachings are the only real truth about the Bible." And Walter Martin, in *Kingdom of the Cults* states, about the Mormons: "One can search the corridors of pagan mythology and never equal the complex structure which the Mormons have erected and masked under the terminology and misnomer of orthodox Christianity."

Question 5 When you discuss the first aspect of a cult, its distortion of Christ, this would include denial of the doctrine of the Trinity, denial of His bodily resurrection, and erroneous views about His Second Coming. Errors about Christ are the most serious because He is the key to our salvation and understanding of God (see John 8:24).

Question 7 The main differences are in who Christ is and what saves us. Note: Some of the members of your group may feel

intimidated if they don't know enough about the Bible to make knowledgeable statements. Assure those who are struggling that, at this point in their spiritual journey, it's okay to be learning about this topic and that keeping at it is more important than getting everything perfect.

Question 8 If what you mean by *cult* is a group whose members live radical, out-of-the-mainstream lifestyles, these groups don't fit that definition—members of these groups are found throughout our society. But if by *cult* you mean a group who teaches that it exclusively is Christianity and yet deviates in significant ways from traditional Christian teaching, then both Mormons and Jehovah's Witnesses would fall into that category.

Question 9 Because the Bible is a major source (among others) of the teachings of both Mormons and Jehovah's Witnesses, similarities of moral practice exist. Besides, nowhere in the Bible does it states that only followers of the true faith have external goodness. Lots of people live exemplary lives—even atheists. What's missing from anyone outside of the sphere of Christ is forgiveness of sin.

Question 10 Jesus was also referring to the effects of their doctrinal teachings. A false prophet could gather followers and turn them into nice people who defer to the cult leader for truth instead of Christ and the Bible. These people are therefore lost spiritually even though they're good people externally.

Question 11 To label a religion as a cult or sect is not spiritual bigotry if the designation is made after careful examination of the teachings of that religion. Also, bigotry assumes you're saying something unfair about someone's character. Labeling a group a spiritual counterfeit says nothing about the moral qualities of the people in that group, only about its teachings.

Question 13 Ongoing, healthy questioning of one's own beliefs is a good thing. We believe it is crucial to carefully examine the teachings behind Christianity in order to gain confidence and assurance that Christianity is truly from God. By continually testing the claims of any church or leader (including our own) against the Bible, we can have reasonable certainty of what we believe. There is no room for smug or glib confidence about spiritual matters; our lives must be based on a continuing examination and reexamination of truth.

Session 5: Is Jesus Really the Only Way to God?

Short Answer: Yes. Jesus Christ claimed to be the only one who, through His death and resurrection, is able to forgive sinners and bring people into a relationship with God.

Questions 1 and 2 There are a number of reasons people cannot accept that Jesus Christ is the only way to God, perhaps the strongest being that there so many people who do not believe in Jesus Christ who would therefore be excluded from God. The exclusivity of Christianity troubles many people because it seems unfair to deny those who believe differently access to God and His blessings.

Question 5 Some people assume that only Christians—not Christ, and not the Bible—claim Jesus is the only way to God. This question is designed to expose this misunderstanding by looking at the Scriptures, which clearly teach that Jesus and the Bible make that astonishing claim.

Question 7 Here are the corresponding assumptions matched to each objection listed in the Straight Talk "Three Common Objections": (1) popular opinion defines truth; (2) intensity of belief insures truth; and (3) anything too intolerant negates truth.

Question 8 The illustrations given in the Straight Talk "Common Assumptions Examined" clearly show that the cultural assumptions about truth are not correct. There is no good reason to accept these erroneous assumptions in the spiritual realm, either.

Question 9 This question is a follow-up to the Paul Little quote above. Because Jesus specifically claimed that He was the only way to God, the only logical conclusions are that Jesus was either a liar, a lunatic, a made-up legend, or the truth. If He is not the truth, then the only possible conclusions are the three remaining ones listed above.

Question 10 If there is more than one way to God, then Christ's death was not really necessary. In a sense, He died in vain, because there were other ways to God all along. But the Bible claims just the opposite, that Jesus died and rose again because it was the only hope of the world. Sin must be dealt with, and Christ is the way God bridged the "sin gap."

Question 11 If a person were a true Christian but believed there were other ways to God besides through Jesus, that person would be a Christian in spite of that belief, certainly not because of it. All Christians contain a certain amount of error (you *do* know that about yourself, don't you?), so a person could be mistaken about what other people need even if he or she is personally trusting in Christ. Over time, that person would surely come to see that the Christ he or she was depending on said the things He said, and to continue to reject those statements would be a problem that needed to be fixed. This question could stir some interesting discussion in your group!

Question 12 Use this question to help your group members come to grips with their own relationship with God and with talking to others about knowing Him. Members of your group may want to actually take the step of asking Christ into their lives at this point in the series. Others may begin to take seriously their need to figure out how to creatively share the Christian message with friends and family.

Session 6: What Happens to People Who've Never Heard of Jesus?

Short Answer: The bulk of biblical evidence suggests people are lost without Christ, so we need to bring His message to them. After all, did you need Christ? Would some other way have worked for you? If you clearly needed Christ, what makes you think other people don't?

Questions 1 and 2 Some people believe that as long as they don't know about the truth, they won't be held responsible for it. In that view, ignorance is an excuse that relieves people of any moral obligation to seek truth. Use these questions to get your group members to debate this issue.

Question 3 If it were really true that ignorance implies innocence, then it would be a mistake to send missionaries to expose people to a knowledge that would put them at risk. It would be a waste of the missionary's life to engage in such activity, especially if the missionary were exposed to any danger. It is interesting to note that the Bible clearly teaches that we are to go and make known the Christian message to everyone in the world, even if it requires great personal sacrifice. Why would that be necessary if people are doing fine without the gospel?

Question 4 R. C. Sproul is making the point that innocent people who are without sin don't exist—which is what the Bible also clearly teaches (see Romans 3:9–18). Everyone needs a Savior, whether they've heard about Jesus or not. He's saying the question has to be changed to, "What happens to *guilty* people who have never heard of Jesus Christ?"

Question 5 The Bible doesn't teach that people are condemned for rejecting the Christian message; it teaches that people are condemned because they are sinners, and that rejecting the Christian message is just one more sin—not the sole act which condemns them. R. C. Sproul agrees: ". . . if the remote native is guilty, wherein lies his guilt? Is he punished for not believing in a Christ of whom he never heard? If God is just, that cannot be the case. If God were to punish a person for not responding to a message he had no possibility of hearing, that would be gross injustice; it would be radically inconsistent with God's own revealed justice. We can rest assured that no one is ever punished for rejecting Christ if they've never heard of Him. Before we sigh too deep a breath of relief, let us keep in mind that the native is still not off the hook. . . It is precisely at this point that the New Testament locates the universal guilt of man . . . God's wrath is revealed not against innocence or ignorance but against ungodliness and wickedness" (*Reason to Believe*).

Questions 6 and 7 These verses teach that all people have enough information to know that God exists and that they need Him in their lives. The failure to respond to that inner prompting means they are without excuse, regardless of whether they've heard about Jesus. People who die separated *by their own choice* from God stay separated from God in eternity.

Questions 9 and 10 Because people in your small group have obviously heard about Jesus, technically these questions don't pertain to them. In some cases, this question is used by people as a kind of smoke screen to avoid dealing with the claims of Christianity on a personal level. We can be certain God is just, that no one will ever wind up in hell shaking their fist at God, yelling, "Unfair, unfair!" Assure those who are wondering what God is like that because of Jesus and what the Bible says, we know He is good and just, even if some aspects of these questions perplex us.

Question 12 You may wish to use this question to help members of your group discuss ways to reach out to others.

Do Science and the Bible Conflict?

Session 1: Isn't Christianity Based on Blind Faith?

Short Answer: No, it's based on facts mixed with informed faith (not blind faith) to produce a new life in Christ.

Questions 1 through 4 These questions will get people talking about how their background has predisposed them to various perspectives on science and faith, including gross misconceptions about either.

Question 5 Calling Christianity a faith doesn't mean it doesn't have evidence to back it up. Lots of things aren't science, but we couldn't live without them (marriage, love, parenting, even life itself). Even the great scientist Albert Einstein once said, "No, this trick won't work . . . How on earth are you ever going to explain in terms of chemistry and physics so important a biological phenomenon as first love?" To be a science, it would have to be a field of study open to repeatable experiments and theorizing about phenomena in the observable universe.

Question 6 Christianity is based on facts, though it uses faith to activate and make personal what facts have established. For example, salvation is based on the historic fact of Jesus dying for our sins—no amount of faith can make that real if it didn't really happen. However, once we come to know that it did happen, we receive the gift of salvation by faith (trusting that God to do what He promised through Christ He would do).

Question 7 Not only is it good to know we can be mistaken, it's good to know what gives us our confidence and what could erode that confidence. If a group member is closed-minded, that should come out in the response to this question.

Question 9 Even someone as great a theologian as Martin Luther said it was not wise to believe something that contradicts Scripture or reason. At his trial for heresy, he said, "Reason is not our enemy, but neither is it without limits." That's why we need revelation and illumination to complete the picture of how we can gain spiritual knowledge.

Question 10 Trust is essential for any relationship to work. Many people have a problem with trust that affects all their relationships, not just their relationship with God. Those who have difficulty trusting get upset if they're asked to trust God. The true problem is their trust issue, not the requirement to trust God.

For others, it is difficult to trust in God because He is a person so different than us—invisibility being one such difference that makes for a big problem in the relationship! But trusting is not impossible. God has provided many helps for our spiritual life (the wonders of creation, the Bible, other believers, and Jesus, to name a few).

Question 11 Some people don't like to have to think, because it's work. But it's important that we all know why we believe, and we are commanded in the Bible to "be prepared to give an answer to everyone who asks you to give the reason for the hope that you have" (1 Peter 3:15).

Question 12 Everyone has faith. Even the scientist has faith in his instruments, faith that the scientific method will give him results, faith that he will find order in the universe that makes science meaningful. The key is not to eliminate faith, but to be sure your faith—in whatever area of life—has a worthy object at all times. C. S. Lewis' definition of faith found in *Christian Reflections*, a collection of essays, may be helpful at this point: "Faith is the power of continuing to believe what we once honestly thought to be true until cogent reasons for honestly changing our minds are brought before us."

Session 2: Why Are So Few Scientists Christians?

Short Answer: Currently the field of science is biased toward materialistic atheism, but that has not always been the case.

Question 2 Many people have had the experience of religion being forced on them at an early age. Such an approach probably damaged the credibility of Christianity, even though the fault was with a system that didn't allow for questions and with insecure teachers who wouldn't allow themselves to be questioned. Assure group members, especially the seekers in your group, that such dogmatism and narrow-mindedness is not part of your group experience, and that it isn't how biblical Christianity is supposed to be.

Question 3 This statement is a gross simplification. Scientists have a kind of faith, and religion—at least Christianity—is meaningless without facts.

Question 5 Although it's true that, as a rule, scientists are encouraged to be objective, scientists have a desire and vested interest in being right. And if they're committed to a point of view, say, nontheistic evolution, scientists may do amazing intellectual contortions to hang on to a theory. R. C. Sproul wrote about one essay he read from a well-known Nobel Prize-winning scientist. In that article the scientist argued that the idea of "spontaneous generation"—life from nonlife, with no cause—should be abandoned in science once and for all. He then proposed a new model: gradual spontaneous generation. Sproul was incredulous. "How can something gradual be spontaneous? How can something spontaneous be gradual? Our scientist wanted to debunk the myth that something can come *suddenly* from nothing and replace it with a better myth that something can come *gradually* from nothing." As Sproul noted, "even the most astute scientists can nod. They can fall asleep at the switch and be suddenly very unscientific in their pronouncements" (R. C. Sproul, *Lifeviews*).

Consider also what the renowned atheistic scientist Carl Sagan once said: "If we must worship a power greater than ourselves, does it not make sense to revere the sun and the stars? Hidden within every astronomical investigation, sometimes so deeply buried that the researcher himself is unaware of its presence, is a kernel of awe." The apostle Paul was right on the mark: "For although they knew God, they neither glorified him as God nor gave thanks to him. . . . They exchanged the truth of God for a lie, and worshiped and served created things rather than the Creator" (Romans 1:21, 25).

Finally, if you think scientists are completely impartial, just attend some scientific convention or symposium—you will see plenty of "ego" mixed in with the facts!

Question 6 The big difference between openness to God and openness to tooth fairies is the comparative amount of evidence for either. Clearly, in science, history, and human experience there is far more going for belief in God than belief in tooth fairies.

Question 7 Science doesn't tell us one way or the other if the supernatural exists. If a scientist makes a statement that he doesn't believe in anything supernatural, that is a nonscientific statement. If a scientist says science can explain everything, that too is a philosophical statement, not a scientific one. As J. P. Moreland observed, "Science cannot be practiced in thin air. In fact, science itself presupposes a number of substantive philosophical theses that must be assumed if science is even to get off the runway. Each of these assumptions has been challenged, and the task of stating and defending these assumptions is one of the tasks of philosophy. The conclusions of science cannot be more certain than the presuppositions it rest on and uses to reach those conclusions" (*The Creation Hypothesis*).

Question 9 The resurrection of Jesus is an historical question, not a scientific one. To rule out the possible involvement of God is not a scientific statement, it is a philosophical one—and a very biased one at that, because it sets aside a reasonable option before even examining the evidence.

Question 10 Pure science just observes, formulates hypotheses, and tests them. Calling everything else subjective is not a scientific statement (science doesn't tell you "everything except science is subjective"; your philosophical bent tells you that).

Question 12 Some people think that to believe in God will introduce a bias in scientific inquiry. To an extent, it may. But having a view of God, and knowing you have that view, is an honest way to approach a study. It is actually more objective than determining beforehand, without examining any evidence, what could *not* possibly be true on the basis of an unadmitted materialistic bias.

Question 13 Obviously, any attempt to distort theology to fit current "science" is doomed to look silly at some point in the future. God's revelation, even if it poses problems to modern scientific theory, is not foolishness, and will ultimately be vindicated.

Session 3: Doesn't the Big Bang Disprove a Creator?

Short Answer: No, it is actually strong evidence for a God outside of time and space who created everything—a fact many cosmologists recognize.

Questions 2 and 3 It is important for group members to state early on in the discussion what they know about this theory. Some may be very well-read, while others have little or no technical knowledge. Obviously, those with less knowledge should not make dogmatic statements!

Question 5 Along these lines, Robert Griffiths, a Heinemann recipient in mathematical physics, once joked, "If we need an atheist for a debate, I go to the philosophy department. The physics department isn't much use" (quoted by Hugh Ross in *The Creator and the Cosmos*).

Question 6 That all the galaxies were once condensed into an infinitely small point is, humanly speaking, incomprehensible, but cosmologists regularly describe that as factual. It's amazing how science can ask us to imagine such amazing realities, yet mock religion for its "mysteries." Truly, the universe is a complex place, so simple answers to religion or science are not always forthcoming. Spiritual teachers should be respected even when they describe things difficult to grasp.

Question 7 People are often threatened by what they don't know. Christians who feel attacked by modern science may attempt to gain easy answers in order to defend themselves or to not feel stupid. A more honest approach is to admit we don't know as much as we wish we did, and to do some homework in areas that interest us. Otherwise, it makes sense—and seems the honest thing to do—to be quiet and listen more.

Questions 10 and 11 It's hard to understand why anyone would do anything other than seek their own well-being if we are all just a cosmic accident. "One can cannot get 'ought' from 'is,' and that's what naturalism requires us to do. In short, naturalism fails to give a foundation for one of the deepest issues of human life—the issues of life and death itself. If naturalism is true, there can be no justice on the basis of an objective standard that measures all human beings. There can only be the adjudication of power: physical power, rhetorical power, political power, social power (i.e., the power of tradition) or charismatic power (i.e., the persuasive power of personality)" (James Sire, "How can I know that what I believe is true?" posted on the Internet, Mars Hill Forum).

Stepping on an ant, committing murder, and junking a car are essentially identical actions if we aren't beings created in God's image. A person's view of where we came from has enormous consequences on what that person does with his or her life.

Session 4: Doesn't Evolution Contradict Genesis?

Short Answer: Yes, but materialistic evolution is probably not the best explanation for the origin of life; misinterpreting Genesis also leads to problems explaining how life began.

Question 3 Very few people who believe in evolution can point out any weaknesses to the theory. That seems odd, because thorough study of any subject should include study of counter-arguments. One professor who observed this one-sided education described a sample conversation with one of his students: "He would take it rather badly when I suggested that he was not being very scientific in his outlook if he swallowed the latest scientific dogma and, when questioned, just repeated parrot-fashion the views of the current Archbishop of Evolution. In fact, he would be behaving like certain of those religious students he affected to despise. He would be taking on faith what he could not intellectually understand and, when questioned, would appeal to authority of a 'good book,' which in this case was *The Origin of Species*" (quoted in *Know Why You Believe* by Paul Little).

Question 4 Again, listen for what level of knowledge people have about this subject. Challenge those on either side of this issue who want to make sweeping statements that they need good facts to back up what they say.

Question 6 Most people fear that if evolution were true, life didn't get here through a God who created. Also, the authority of the Bible is questioned. Clearly, whoever wrote Genesis 1 and 2 had no idea what they were talking about. If it's just a made-up fable, what else in the Bible could be made up as well? On the other side, if God did create us, a believer in evolution will have to modify his or her belief system which, up to now, has assumed we're an accident caused by chance.

Question 7 (The following paragraphs come from Norman Geisler, President of Southern Evangelical Seminary, in the article "Darwin's Black Box: A Brief Review," posted on the Internet.)

The most recent and hottest attack on Darwinism comes form Michael Behe, Associate Professor of Biochemistry

at Lehigh University in *Darwin's Black Box*, NY: The Free Press, 1996.

The thesis of the book is very simple: 1) Irreducible complexity cannot be accounted for by small incremental changes; 2) Life, especially on the molecular level, is often irreducibly complex; 3) Therefore, Darwinism has no explanation for such life.

Further, 1) irreducible complexity is best accounted for by intelligent design; 2) such irreducible complexity exit in living cells; 3) Hence, the best explanation for such life is an intelligent Designer.

Darwin admitted: "If it could be demonstrated that any complex organ existed which could not possibly have been formed by numerous, successive, slight modifications, my theory would absolutely breakdown" (Darwin Origin of Species, 6th ed. NYU, 1988, p. 154).

Evolutionist Richard Dawkins agrees: "Evolution is very possibly not, in actual fact, always gradual. But it must be gradual when it is being used to explain the coming into existence of complicated, apparently designed objects, like eyes. For if it is not gradual in these cases, it ceases to have any explanatory power at all. Without gradualness in these cases, we are back to miracle, which is a synonym for the total absence of [naturalistic] explanation" (Dawkins, *River Out of Eden*, 83).

[Challenges Behe:] "No one at Harvard University, no one at the National Institutes of Health, no member of the National Academy of Sciences, no Nobel prize winner—no one at all can give a detailed account of how the cilium, or vision, or blood clotting, or any complex biochemical process might have developed in a Darwinian fashion. But we are here. All these things got here somehow; if not in a Darwinian fashion, then how?" (Behe, *Darwin's Black Box*, 187).

Question 8 This question may generate some heated discussion because it strikes close to home for believers who have a high view of Scripture. Some interpreters are *extremely* uncomfortable with taking any statements in Genesis poetically; for them, if Genesis says there was "evening and morning," then there were twenty-four hours and there was a evening and a morning (even though the sun was yet to be created!). Our view is that Genesis is an accurate description of the creation of the universe and of life but leaves out many details that would interest a scientist. It only makes sense that God would describe how He made the world and us in terms that any culture or education level could understand. He knew getting bogged down in scientific precision would lose multitudes of readers with no access to that knowledge, so He revealed His work in broad strokes so that we'd all be clear about the "who" and "what," but not necessarily the "how" (see next session for more on this).

Question 11 It must terrify someone who is committed to rejecting God when evidence for His existence emerges! Likewise, a believer is probably frightened when it appears his or her belief is unfounded. No one likes to be wrong; no one wants to look foolish. This is especially true when it comes to such monumental beliefs as where we came from and who made us.

Session 5: If the Bible Is True, Why Isn't It More Scientific?

Short Answer: The Bible is aimed at all societies and all education levels, so it uses the language of observation rather than precise scientific terminology. Besides, science changes so rapidly that any scientific description would be outdated in a few years, making the Bible sound silly.

Question 2 Some people make a split between relying on the Bible for spiritual truth and believing what it says about "secular" issues—like history, for example. Such a split is not honest, however, because spiritual truth and history are inextricably intertwined. God revealed Himself in history, and Jesus was a man of history who provided for salvation at a point in history. Our faith is invalid if the Bible's historic claims are erroneous. Besides, why would you trust a source for truths you couldn't prove (spiritual ones) when you found it was corrupt in other areas where you *could* test it (history)?

Question 5 It may not totally destroy a person's faith to discover an archaeological contradiction because it is always possible that we haven't understood correctly what the archaeological find means. Still, to be consistent, we would have to grant that a known contradiction between the Bible and archaeology would effectively erode our faith in the Bible as reliable and as a truth source from God.

Question 7 Estimates *can* be false if they are way off. But they're not false if they're estimates and taken as such. Language that

is not precise can be right or wrong, but it is not automatically wrong just because it's imprecise. God gives us lots of pictures of how much He loves us—is it a problem that He does so without scientific precision?

Question 9 If a person has an ax to grind, finding so-called contradictions can be one way to get back at the religion or religious person who made the person mad. That person needs to be more honest about what is gong on, and to stop attacking the Bible when something else is the real issue.

Question 10 The theological term used to describe this is "to condescend" and it is a good way to picture what God has to do to speak to us on our finite, limited level. He must get truth down to us on our level, and by taking on our form of communication He will necessarily be constrained by its limitations. The amazing thing is how well His revelation does work, in spite of the limits of language. And of course, by sending the Word incarnate, He has made Himself very clear: "In the past God spoke to our forefathers through the prophets at many times and in various ways, but in these last days he has spoken to us by his Son, whom he appointed heir of all things, and through whom he made the universe. The Son is the radiance of God's glory and the exact representation of his being..." (Hebrews 1:1–3).

Session 6: Won't the Progress of Science Make God Unnecessary?

Short Answer: No, because science has its limits and belief in God isn't based on the observations of science. The evidence for God is positive; He's not just the explanation for things science doesn't know yet.

Question 2 It's easy to be impressed with advances in science because they are so startling and beneficial. But when we look at the human condition, at war and oppression and dysfunction everywhere you turn, optimism about science solving all our problems seems far too idealistic.

Questions 3, 4, and 5 Our belief in God will not hold up to scrutiny if it is based merely on what we can't explain with science. Jesus gives us *positive* evidence to help us believe in God, rather than falling to the trap of basing our theism merely on the absence of a reasonable alternative to a scientific theory.

Question 8 Although this guide (and series) comes to a close with this session, you as the leader should pay attention to what people in your group, especially seekers, say here. At a minimum, it would help to have follow-up conversations about these topics, and it may make sense to have the whole group explore some of the issues together.

Question 10 C. S. Lewis, a former atheist turned believer, pointed out that "just as the Christian has his moments when the clamor of this visible and audible world is so persistent and the whisper of the spiritual world so faint that faith and reason can hardly stick to their guns, so, as I well remember, the atheist too has his moments of shuddering misgiving, of an all but irresistible suspicion that old tales may after all be true, that something or someone from outside may at any moment break into his neat, explicable, mechanical universe. Believe in God and you will have to face hours when it seems *obvious* that this material world is the only reality; disbelieve in Him and you must face hours when this material world seems to shout at you that it is not all" ("Religion: Reality or Substitute?" in *Christian Reflections*).

Why Become a Christian?

Session 1: Why Would Anyone Think I'm Not a Christian?

Short Answer: Contrary to popular belief, being a Christian is not a matter of religious performance; it is a matter of a new spiritual birth—being "born again."

Question 2 It is certainly possible to have a false sense of security about being a Christian. The Bible abounds with warnings against spiritual presumption (see next Straight Talk). Some people in your group may define being a Christian differently than the Bible does. Those people may still be Christians (despite their erroneous definitions), but they need to know the truth about what it actually means to be a Christ follower. And of course, some in your group may think they are believers but are not. The tough questions posed in this session are so important because people's eternal destiny is at stake.

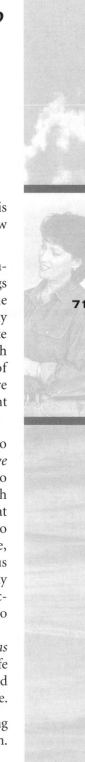

71

Question 3 As soon as people start pointing to things they do as proof they're Christians, they confuse what it takes to *live as* a Christian and what it takes to *become* a Christian. Two people who are not married could walk arm-in-arm, kiss each other, even go to the same home at the end of the day—but that doesn't make them married. A day must come when they go beyond dating and proclaim unreservedly "I do." Likewise, people can be associated with spirituality and live out various Christian behaviors without encountering Christ in a saving way (it happens to people in cults all the time). So the definitive factor of being a Christian cannot be lifestyle related—it has to relate in some way to receiving Christ.

Having said that, we would expect that someone who *has* encountered Christ to live an obedient life. But an obedient life doesn't save the person—it is simply evidence that Jesus showed up and is making His presence known through the person's life.

Questions 4, 5, and 6 None of the activities listed (including being born into a Christian family) qualifies a person to be a Christian.

Those activities are things that most likely would be a part of a Christian's lifestyle *as a result of* receiving Jesus as forgiver and leader, but none of them are what makes a person a Christian. A person crosses the line to become a Christian by receiving Jesus as the forgiver of sins and new leader of his or her life.

Question 7 The key to this question is Jesus' phrase, "I never knew you." To *know* someone in the biblical sense is to have an intimate relationship. (The verb *to know* is sometimes used in place of the word *sex*, the zenith of human intimacy.) Jesus rejected those who associated with spiritual activities and spiritually minded people, but who never had a connection—a personal relationship—with Jesus. Of course, being omniscient, He knew who they were. He knew everything about them. But He never *knew* them personally. So regardless of what those people did, there was no spiritual life or salvation present in them, and therefore they were still lost in sin.

Question 8 A true Christian is one who has at some point accepted Jesus Christ as the only way to be forgiven for sin. As a result of receiving that tremendous gift, a Christian places his or her life gratefully into God's hands. That gratitude is expressed a variety of ways, among them: worship, godly character development, service, fellowship with other Christians, spiritual growth, sharing one's faith, and honoring God in every area of life.

Question 9 The term "born again" is another way of communicating that a person has to choose to *become* a Christian—not *ooze* his or her way in. It implies that accepting Christ is a beginning, a start of a whole new life in Christ (see 2 Corinthians 5:17). John R. W. Stott puts it this way in his book *Basic Christianity*, "But whatever his parentage and upbringing, every responsible adult is obliged to make up his own mind for or against Christ. We cannot remain neutral. Nor can we drift into Christianity. Nor can anyone else settle the matter for us. We must decide for ourselves."

Question 10 The fact that someone is religious does not necessarily mean the person is truly a Christian. Nicodemus apparently counted on his religiosity, and Jesus and warned him that to do so was a false assumption. Religious people tend to take their stand on their heritage, and Jesus made it clear the only way for someone to understand true spirituality is to consider your "religiousness" worthless and begin to think in terms of starting all over again.

The apostle Paul realized he needed to be born again in spite of his religious heritage. He wrote of himself,

> If anyone else thinks he has reasons to put confidence in the flesh, I have more: circumcised on the eighth day, of the people of Israel, of the tribe of Benjamin, a Hebrew of Hebrews; in regard to the law, a Pharisee; as for zeal, persecuting the church; as for legalistic righteousness, faultless. But whatever was to my profit I now consider loss for the sake of Christ. What is more, I consider everything a loss compared to the surpassing greatness of knowing Christ Jesus my Lord, for whose sake I have lost all things. I consider them rubbish, that I may gain Christ and be found in him, not having a righteousness of my own that comes from the law, but that which is through faith in Christ— the righteousness that comes from God and is by faith.
> —Philippians 3:4–9

Questions 11 and 12 Please use these questions to assist your group members to take a hard look at their own lives to see where they personally stand with Jesus Christ. Be sensitive to the fact they may each be at different places and may need your individual counsel to help determine their next steps.

Session 2: Why All This Talk About Sin?

Short Answer: Dismissing sin as irrelevant or without consequence is spiritually fatal. While it may be true that some believers are negative people who cloak their irascibility with spiritual language, it's hard to imagine how warning people of the eternal consequence of their rebellion against God could be considered too negative.

Question 2 The central human dilemma is spiritual rebellion against God, not ignorance of Him. Because of God's revelation of Himself through creation and conscience, we have more knowledge of Him than we might think—enough to make us "without excuse" (Romans 1:18–20; 2:12–16).

Question 4 Sin is any disobedience against God—any failure to "hit the mark" of His standard, whether that be active rebellion or passive indifference. Sin is the desire to turn away from God in any area of life and leave Him out of out the matter. The repercussions of sin are the immediate loss of God's presence and guidance (spiritual death) and that same loss forever (eternal death, or what the Bible calls "the second death" [Revelation 20:6, 14]).

Question 6 To be spiritually dead means to exist without connection to God and to be under His judgment. It means being without access to the Kingdom of God, though still physically alive with access to God's physical world.

Questions 7 and 8 According to the Bible, the very act of being indifferent or neutral toward God is a way of telling Him you are your own god. If you lived in a kingdom and the king asked if you were one of his citizens but you replied you weren't tied to anyone else, he would undoubtedly keep questioning you until you declared where your loyalties lay. Your "neutrality" could well be considered treason, especially if you were taking advantage of the benefits of the king's kingdom without any commitment to it. To live in God's world yet to declare that the King of that world has no say over your affairs—even if you haven't declared yourself at war with Him—leaves you guilty of the same offense.

By virtue of God's greatness and lordship over all of His creation, He deserves our devotion and submission to His leadership. Failure to give it—even though open revolt hasn't been declared—denies Him that position and greatly offends Him.

Question 9 Because God initiated a costly plan to redeem all of us who were separated from Him, we know that it is He who greatly longs for us to come back to Him—much more than we want Him. In addition, by sending us prophets and His written Word, and by working on every one of us through the convicting ministry of the Holy Spirit (John 16:7–8), He is clearly the original "seeker."

Question 10 Any of us can find someone who makes us feel superior. But the standard by which we measure ourselves needs to be Jesus Christ Himself.

Question 11 No amount of good we can muster can make up for the loss incurred by sin. It's like telling someone dying of two punctured lungs to get better by breathing harder or faster. It might do some good for a short while, but it won't heal the wound or save the person's life.

Question 12 Once a person honestly comes to grips with personal sin, there should be a deep sense of regret and sorrow at the realization of the blatant insult that sin is to God. We should want to resolve the situation—and do it *God's* way—as soon as possible. Healthy fear can lead to accepting God's grace and love, which in turn provides great peace and hope for the future.

Question 14 Use the answers to this question to follow-up with members in your group on an individual basis. What an exciting thing it would be to assist someone in your group to realize he or she needs and wants Jesus Christ to provide forgiveness and new life! There's no greater privilege than to be used by God to help someone cross the line and invite Jesus into his or her life.

Session 3: Why Can't I Make It On My Own?

Short Answer: Because no one has what it takes; God expects moral perfection, and any sin—*only one*—makes that forever impossible.

Question 2 Some people believe they have no sin problem and, as a result, see no need for forgiveness. Jesus said He came to call on those who are sick, not on those who are well. To change the analogy slightly, in reality we're all blind, but as soon as we think we have sight, we stop looking for a cure . . . and remain spiritually blind (Jesus said this very thing to the Pharisees in John 9:40–41).

Question 3 When we give a free gift, we get joy out of seeing someone receive and enjoy that gift. But if they offer us something for that gift—especially if what they offer is paltry compared to what the gift is really worth—the offer can feel like an insult. Considering the fact that Jesus paid for salvation with His blood, how ridiculous does it look for us to think we can offer God our "good works" as payment? How close do our attempts at goodness come to His perfection and purity?

Question 4 God provided His Son, an innocent lamb without blemish or defect, as the perfect sacrifice able to make payment for the sins of the world. Cliffe Knechtle summarizes things this way: "God is just, holy and morally perfect. We all stand guilty before God because we fall far short of his perfection. But the Bible also reveals that God is loving and merciful. He has provided a way to escape the condemnation we deserve. He has sent his Son to die for us."

Question 5 The two biggest reasons are pride and disbelief. Pride says, "I can do it myself, I don't need your help. I don't want to have to be indebted to you, God." Disbelief says, "I know Jesus said He paid it all, but I can't believe it's that easy. There must be a catch, so I'll take precautions rather than trust His promise."

Question 7 A wage is something you earn and is due you; a gift is something someone else gives you that is not tied to performance in any way.

Questions 8, 9, 10, and 11 These questions are designed to help you as the leader discern where your group members are in their spiritual journey. Please pay special attention to indications your group members may give concerning their readiness to personally accept Jesus Christ as forgiver and leader. Of course, the decision to receive Christ must not be coerced in any way, but when the time is right, you may wish to invite members to do this through prayer—even during the session if it seems appropriate.

Session 4: Why Is Jesus So Important?

Short Answer: Jesus is the only one able to forgive our sins because He alone paid the price: His life in exchange for ours.

Question 1 Of course God is omniscient and hears our prayers—in that sense we don't need to go through Jesus to get to God (Satan directly goes to God in this sense—see Job 1:6). But God sees our sin, and therefore cannot have *fellowship* with us. It is only when Christ takes away the guilt and substitutes His righteousness in us that God can now connect with us and have a close relationship.

Question 3 Answers will probably vary. Let them all stand for now, because the Straight Talk that follows will help make this more clear.

Questions 4, 5, and 6 The purpose behind the death of Jesus was to make payment for the sins of the world. The Bible makes it clear that the penalty of sin is death. We all have a choice: we can either make that payment ourselves (which leads to eternal separation from God) or accept the payment Jesus Christ made on our behalf (which leads to eternal life with God in His Kingdom). Jesus' death on the cross is sufficient to make payment for our sins because He, being God, was without any sin Himself. He alone was able to pay the full price. No other religion offers a complete pardon of sin; they all offer either some program for human achievement, or a God who overlooks sin and is therefore not holy. "If Jesus were not fully God, He *could* not be our Savior. But if He were God and yet did nothing on our behalf—that is, did not *do* something to bring us to God—He *would* not be our Savior. Being God *qualified* Jesus Christ to be Savior, but His atoning death for us *made* Him our Savior. Jesus not only *could* save men; He *did*" (Paul Little, *Know What You Believe*).

Questions 7, 8, and 9 Because Jesus was fully human, He wrestled with the choice to give up His life as a sacrifice on our behalf. He loved and trusted the Father, and He loved those His death would save, but the pain and spiritual torment of taking upon Himself the sins of the world was nonetheless real—and agonizing. This struggle can be an example for us by showing us we need to do the right thing even when it's hard to do so. It can also be a comfort to know that just because we've decided something is right, it doesn't mean it will be easy.

Question 10 The resurrection is proof that Jesus is no ordinary man. In all of history—among all other religious leaders—it establishes Him as the supreme source of truth. It is proof that our sin did not overwhelm Him but is forgivable because He overcame it through coming back to life. As Paul Little explains, "The implications of the Resurrection are enormous. We should understand them as fully as possible—and *enjoy* them. First, the Resurrection fully confirms the truth and value of what Jesus taught and did . . . Because of the Resurrection, we know we are not trusting in a myth; we know that our sins are actually forgiven through the death of Christ. Certainty and forgiveness are based on the empty tomb! Christ is the only One who has ever come back from death to tell men about the beyond. In *His* words we know we have the authoritative Word of God Himself" (*Know What You Believe*).

Session 5: Can Someone Like Me Really Change?

Short Answer: Because God provides His followers with new life and a new source of power, even *you* can change!

Question 3 It is common for people to think that they will not be accepted by God until they somehow clean up their act first. It is a humbling thing to openly come to God, claiming no worthiness of our own. The truth is that God *has* accepted us already; all we have to do is come. Any attempt to clean up our act first is really an attempt to save ourselves—and that it is something we could never do. The only way we can ever come to Him is flaws and all. At that point, Jesus forgives and cleanses us.

Question 4 This marriage analogy can also be taken a step further to point out that getting married means some radical changes are coming—it involves a whole new way of living. In a similar way, receiving Christ means being willing to live life differently—now Christ is the leader and honoring Him needs to take top priority. As Paul Little warns, this is a stumbling block for some: "We need to be reminded that ultimately man's basic problem is not intellectual; it is moral. Once in a while our answer won't satisfy someone. His rejection of the answer doesn't invalidate it. On the other hand, he may be convinced and still not become a Christian. I've had fellows tell me, 'You've answered every one of my questions to my satisfaction.' After thanking them for the flattery I've asked, 'Are you going to become a Christian then?' And they've smiled a little sheepishly, 'Well, no.' 'Why not?' I've inquired. 'Frankly, it would mean too radical a change in my way of life.' Many people are not prepared to let anyone else, including God, run their lives. It's not that they can't believe; but they *won't* believe" (*How To Give Away Your Faith*).

Question 6 Because of our sin, no matter how hard we try, we will always fall short. In this sense, we can never copy the perfect life Jesus lived, though we might want to. But when Jesus comes into our life, He begins to do a work in us. Changes start to occur. He gives us the Holy Spirit to guide us and bring us new convictions. He puts new desires and goals in our hearts. By indwelling in us, He gives us the motivation and strength and power to live a Christ-honoring life.

Question 7 You don't need to do anything *before* becoming a Christian, but in order to become a Christian you need to (1) *admit* you're a sinner in need of forgiveness; (2) *be willing* to turn away from sin and cooperate with God to make changes; (3) *believe* that Jesus completed the work of salvation; and (4) personally *receive* Jesus Christ as forgiver and leader. The great scholar F. F. Bruce agrees: "If there is to be any salvation for [anyone], then, it must be based not on ethical achievement but on the grace of God. What [all people] need alike, in fact, is to have their records blotted out by an act of divine amnesty and to have the assurance of acceptance by God for no merit of their own but by his spontaneous mercy. For this need God has made

provision in Christ. Thanks to his redemptive work, men may find themselves 'in the clear' before God . . . The benefits of the atonement thus procured may be appropriated by faith—and only by faith." Bruce later concludes, "True [Christianity] is not a matter of rules and regulations. God does not deal with people like an accountant, but accepts them freely when they respond to his love, and implants the Spirit of Christ in their hearts so that they may show to others the love they have received from him" (*Paul: Apostle of the Heart Set Free*).

Question 8 The promise of salvation was based entirely on what God does, not on what the person does. That precedent means we too can have a relationship with God based on His perfection, not ours.

Questions 9 and 10 The change begins the moment a person receives Christ into his or her life. It may be a very gradual change, but God begins to do His work immediately. He continues to grow us up in our new faith; our responsibility is to follow Him on a daily basis.

Session 6: How Does Someone Actually Become a Christian?

Short Answer: By receiving Jesus Christ: His provision for sin, His power for living, His indwelling presence forever.

Question 2 Becoming a Christian is a combination of an ongoing process of discovery and conviction and a point-in-time conversion. The specifics of each person's journey vary, but Jesus Himself said you cannot see the Kingdom of God without being born again. Even though a person may not remember a specific point in time when he or she received Christ, Jesus comes in only by invitation. So if Christ is there, He was invited.

Question 3 God hasn't set salvation up that way because to do so would be out of character for Him. Instead, He provides salvation as a gift. He wants people who want Him, so salvation is not a coercive act but an offer. If God gave salvation to those who didn't want it, He would be abrogating their power of choice. That would be a violation of the human dignity He gave to all by virtue of making creatures in His image.

Question 4 Becoming a Christian requires an intentional response because God values our power of choice and wants to honor His commitment to invest us with autonomy.

An unopened present can never benefit the recipient; salvation not accepted is ineffectual. A response to God is the very essence of having a relationship with Him, and a relationship is possible only when both party's wills are respected. If only one will is honored, it's called slavery.

Question 5 To intellectually assent to Christianity would be to acknowledge, as a piece of information, that Jesus came into the world to save sinners. Actual acceptance is receiving that benefit for yourself. Years ago, the Great Blondin, an acrobat, stretched a wire across Niagara Falls and offered to take someone across in a wheelbarrow. There were many who "believed" he could do it, but no takers. To get in the wheelbarrow and actually do it—that's the difference between intellectual assent and actual acceptance.

Question 6 Receiving Jesus means to invite Him into your life so that He comes to dwell in you and all the benefits of His life become yours (John 1:12; 1 Peter 2:24; Revelation 3:20). Receiving a gift is not the same as earning it. Our part in the transaction is to acknowledge and accept it; God's part is to apply it to us upon receipt of it.

Question 8 God doesn't want a universe full of people with right answers; He wants children who love Him. He didn't die to prepare us for some heavenly entrance exam; He died to bring us life—to make possible an eternity of relating together.

Question 9 If correct theology saves you, Satan is a saint—his theology is flawless (James 2:19). Obviously, incorrect theology is no virtue. But if people gather knowledge thinking they are getting closer to God or earning favor in His sight, they are mistaken. Knowledge of God in the biblical sense is not accumulation of information; it is knowledge in the sense of intimacy. If God wants to know us in that sense, it means we are His bride and He wants to have the closest possible union with us, spiritually speaking.

Questions 10 and 11 These two questions are really the bottom line of this session, and perhaps the entire Tough Questions series. Our desire has been that as people were stretched and challenged to express where they were in their spiritual journey, they would eventually come to the point where they would open their lives to the saving work of Christ and cross that line into His kingdom. Please help the members of your group honestly assess what holds them back from making the most important and rewarding decision of their lives. Be in prayer as you gently challenge each person to accept God's wonderful offer of love and forgiveness.

Questions 12 and 13 You may wish to use these questions as a springboard for deciding where your group will head after the completion of this study. Or you may want to follow up individually with each member.

Why Become a Christian?

WILLOW CREEK
RESOURCES

This resource was created to serve you.

It is just one of many ministry tools that are part of the Willow Creek Resources®
line, published by the Willow Creek Association together with Zondervan Publishing
House. The Willow Creek Association was created in 1992 to serve a rapidly growing number of churches from all across the denominational spectrum that are committed to helping unchurched people become fully devoted followers of Christ. There
are now more than 2,500 WCA member churches worldwide.

The Willow Creek Association links like-minded leaders with each other and with
strategic vision, information, and resources in order to build prevailing churches.
Here are some of the ways it does that:

- **Church Leadership Conferences**—3 1/2-day events, held at Willow Creek
  Community Church in South Barrington, IL, that are being used by God to
  help church leaders find new and innovative ways to build prevailing churches
  that reach unchurched people.

- **The Leadership Summit**—a once-a-year event designed to increase the leadership effectiveness of pastors, ministry staff, volunteer church leaders, and Christians in business.

- **Willow Creek Resources**®—to provide churches with a trusted channel of
  ministry resources in areas of leadership, evangelism, spiritual gifts, small
  groups, drama, contemporary music, and more. For more information, call Willow Creek Resources® at 800/876-7335. Outside the US call 610/532-1249.

- *WCA News*—a bimonthly newsletter to inform you of the latest trends,
  resources, and information on WCA events from around the world.

- *The Exchange*—our classified ads publication to assist churches in recruiting
  key staff for ministry positions.

- **The Church Associates Directory**—to keep you in touch with other WCA
  member churches around the world.

- *WillowNet*—an Internet service that provides access to hundreds of Willow
  Creek messages, drama scripts, songs, videos, and multimedia suggestions.
  The system allows users to sort through these elements and download them
  for a fee.

- *Defining Moments*—a monthly audio journal for church leaders, in which Lee
  Strobel asks Bill Hybels and other Christian leaders probing questions to help
  you discover biblical principles and transferable strategies to help maximize
  your church's potential.

For conference and membership information please write or call:

Willow Creek Association   ph: (847) 765-0070
P.O. Box 3188   fax: (847) 765-5046
Barrington, IL 60011-3188   www.willowcreek.org

Select your next Bible study from these Willow Creek and Zondervan series

Walking with God: This bestselling Willow Creek six-book series takes an in-depth look at your relationship with God and your action as a member of His kingdom. Two 500-page leader's guides, each supporting three study guides, ensure thoughtful, informative discussions.

Beatitudes—The Lifestyle God Rewards: This series of eight study guides based on Jesus' Sermon on the Mount covers each of the beatitudes, introducing your group to the ideal of Christian living. Learn how to assume the role of a peacemaker, discover how biblical meekness reaps eternal rewards, and more.

Interactions: Cutting-edge, open-ended series designed to help small group participants develop into fully devoted followers of Christ, and, along the way, deepen their relationship with one another.

Fruit of the Spirit: Each guide covers one fruit of the Spirit: Faithfulness, Gentleness, Joy, Kindness, Love, Patience, Peace, and Self-Control.

Discipleship: Eight study guides introduce key aspects of true Christ-followers: Basic Beliefs, Building Character, Knowing Scripture, New Life in Christ, Sharing Your Faith, Spiritual Disciplines, and Spiritual Warfare.

Great Books of the Bible: Unlock the meaning of the most influential and intriguing books of the Bible, including Ephesians, James, John, Philippians, Proverbs, Psalms, Revelation, and Romans.

Knowing God: Develop intimacy with God by discovering His attributes, His love for His Children, and His power to change lives.

Lifelines: Bible Studies for Students: Four study guides discuss issues important to students, like family relations, loneliness and depression, love, and self-esteem.

Look for these Bible studies at your local Christian bookstore.

ZondervanPublishingHouse
Grand Rapids, Michigan

A Division of HarperCollinsPublishers

WILLOW CREEK
RESOURCES

Tough Questions?
Find the answers with Willow Creek Resources®

The Case for Christ
Lee Strobel

The Project: Determine if there's credible evidence that Jesus of Nazareth really is the Son of God.

The Reporter: Lee Strobel, educated at Yale Law School, award-winning former legal editor of *The Chicago Tribune*—with a background of atheism.

The Experts: A dozen scholars, with doctorates from Cambridge, Princeton, Brandeis, and other top-flight institutions, who are recognized authorities on Jesus.

The Story: Retracing his own spiritual journey, Strobel cross-examines the experts with tough, point-blank questions: How reliable is the New Testament? Does evidence exist for Jesus outside the Bible? Is there any reason to believe the resurrection was an actual historical event? . . .

This colorful, hard-hitting book is no novel. It's a riveting quest for the truth about history's most compelling figure. What will your verdict be in *The Case for Christ?*

Hardcover: 0-310-22646-5
Softcover: 0-310-20930-7

Audio Pages: 0-310-21960-4

Available at your local Christian bookstore.

ZondervanPublishingHouse
Grand Rapids, Michigan
http://www.zondervan.com

A Division of HarperCollinsPublishers

The Journey
NIV

A Bible for Seeking God & Understanding Life

This Bible is designed to draw seekers and new believers into God's Word through practical illustrations that deal with major life issues. Explore a number of themes: Discovering God, Knowing Yourself, Addressing Questions, Strengthening Relationships, Managing Resources, and Reasons to Believe.

Available Now
New International Version

Hardcover	ISBN 0-310-91949-5
Softcover	ISBN 0-310-91950-9
Gospel of John	ISBN 0-310-91951-7

ZondervanPublishingHouse
Grand Rapids, Michigan
http://www.zondervan.com

A Division of HarperCollins*Publishers*

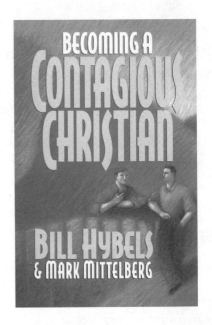

We want to hear from you. Please send your comments about this book to us in care of the address below. Thank you.

ZondervanPublishingHouse
Grand Rapids, Michigan 49530
http://www.zondervan.com